CVC Storybooks
15 Reproducible Emergent Readers

Set 1

I0150467

Stories and Pictures by Mark Linley

bartlebysbox.com

Dedicated to all teachers
and to the children in their care

ISBN 978-0-9977255-0-6

Contact:
    Mark Linley
    bartlebysbox@gmail.com

Dear Teacher,

Hello. My name is Mark Linley, the author and illustrator of the stories in this collection. I am a teacher with eighteen years of teaching experience in the primary grades. I use GUMDROPS for MOPPET TOPS books as a tool in my own classroom, as part of an extensive and well developed systematic early literacy program - a program which I have pieced together and developed myself over the course of my career.

These books have been part of my curriculum for many years and the kids love them. They love the stories, they love the pictures, they love the characters, and they love being able to page through a book and with varying degrees of effort, depending on the child, read every single word. These books work well for children just learning to read, who already know the alphabet and most of the sounds that the letters make. I have personally used these books with pre-kindergartners, kindergartners, beginning first graders, and as extended review for struggling first grade readers. They are easy and appropriate first steps for reading instruction. They will help you to get your students to read.

The GUMDROPS for MOPPET TOPS series was written and illustrated to fill a gap that I saw in the available literature. I created these books because I had students who needed to learn how to blend consonant-vowel-consonant (CVC) words and I was unable to find the right books to address that need. I developed the stories and drew the pictures myself; worked and reworked the drawings by hand and with digital editing software; wrote and rewrote the stories - changing an ending here, moving a page there, discarding stories altogether and writing new ones. These books have gone through many revisions over the years. May they serve you well.

With the GUMDROPS for MOPPET TOPS series, your students will be able read entire books without the frustrating experience of having to puzzle over whether to sound-out a word or to remember it iconically as a sight word. Children feel a sense of accomplishment after successfully reading a page and then moving on to the next page and reading that one too. They feel proud and confident when they are able to read a book by themselves all the way to the end. As a teacher it is a joy to witness the thrill felt by children who have books in their hands that they can read. Finally the kids have books that they can read all the way through!

Enjoy!

Sincerely,

Mark Linley

CONTENTS

PRINTING and ASSEMBLY

I. Copy and Print

For Copy Machines with a Double Sided Printing Option

[OPTION ONE]
Print booklets directly from your GUMDROPS for MOPPET TOPS Blackline Masters Compilation
1. Select two-sided printing on the menu of your copy machine.
2. Open your GUMDROPS for MOPPET TOPS Blackline Masters Compilation to the booklet you wish to print. Scan the page containing the *title page* and *back cover*.
3. Scan the next page in the Compilation, *booklet pages 1* and *10*.
4. Press print to test if both sides of the copy are oriented correctly. If not, re-scan both pages, ensuring that the second page is scanned the other way around.
5. Continue scanning until all pages of your booklet are copied.
6. Press print. All copies will have printed double sided.

[OPTION TWO]
Make MASTER COPIES of your booklets first
1. Copy and print each page of the booklet or booklets your wish to assemble.
2. Place your booklet or booklets in order into the document feeder of your copy machine, *with every other page oriented in the opposite direction*
3. Select the double sided printing option from your machine's menu.
4. Press print. All copies will have printed double sided.

For Copy Machines with a Single Sided Printing Option

A few preliminary *printing tests* will help to determine which way around you must refeed the printed paper for your particular printer or copy machine.

1. Copy and print the odd pages of the booklet you wish to assemble first; print the even pages separately. You will now have two stacks - a stack of odd pages and a stack of even pages.
2. Place the printed odd pages into your copy machine's paper feeder in the direction determined by your printing tests.
3. Place the stack of even pages into the document feeder.
4. Print. Your pages will now be printed double sided.

2. Stack

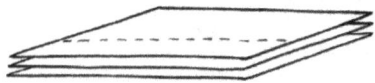

3. Cut

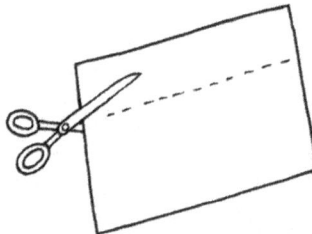

4. Fold and Staple

BOOKLETS

RAT ♡

♡

RAT

RAT

rat   sat
hat   cat

Got it!

Story and Pictures by Mark Linley

GUMDROPS for MOPPET TOPS   SET 1.1

Copyright © 2017 by Mark Linley
All Rights Reserved
MADE IN THE USA

bartlebysbox.com

cut

3

1

cut

rat

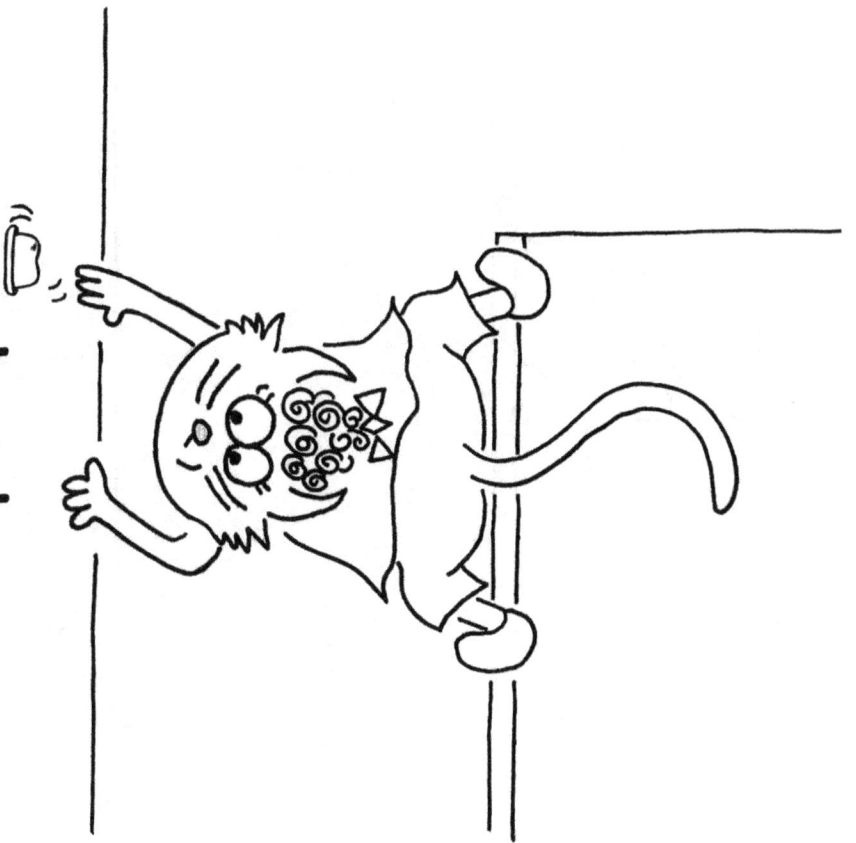

hat

10

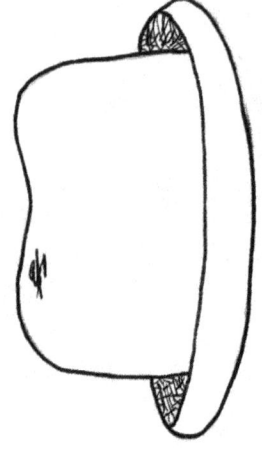

hat

2

cat

9

cut

3

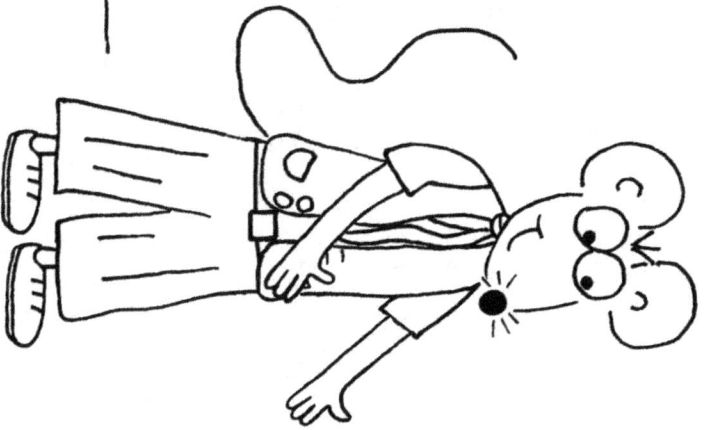

hat

cut

3   8

hat

cut

rat

4

hat

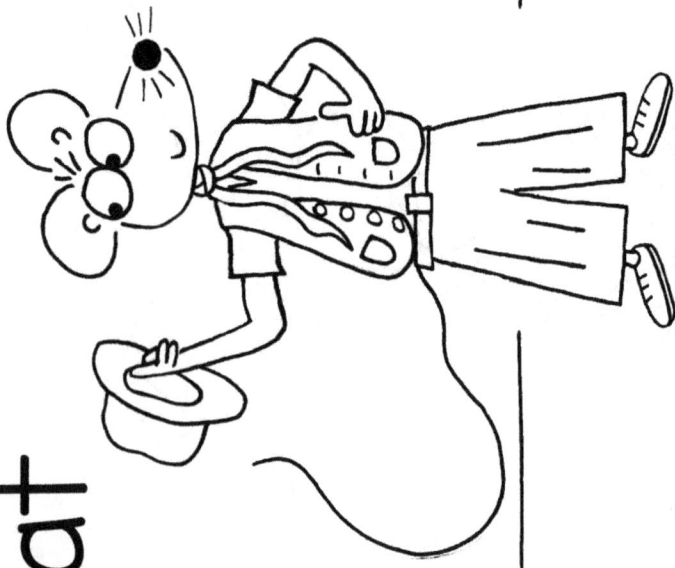

7

5

cut

hat

6

sat

FED

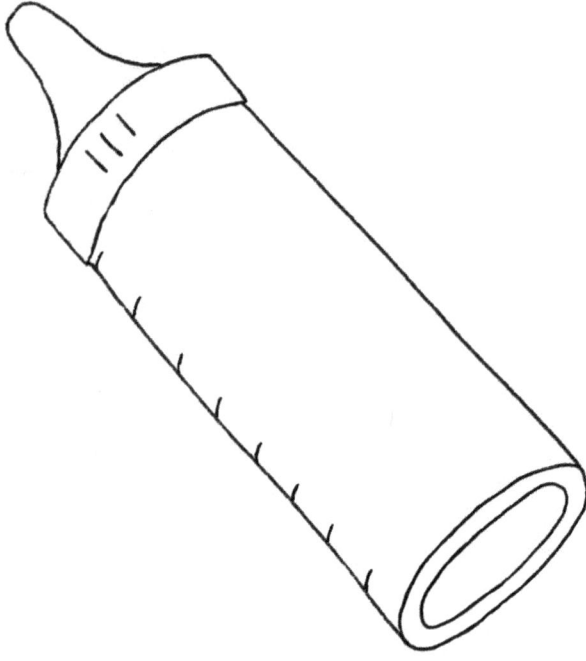

FED

Ted fed
Ned bed
Ed
Jed

Got it!

Story and Pictures by Mark Linley

Copyright © 2017 by Mark Linley
All Rights Reserved
MADE IN THE USA

SET 1.1

GUMDROPS for MOPPET TOPS

bartlebysbox.com

cut

cut

Ted

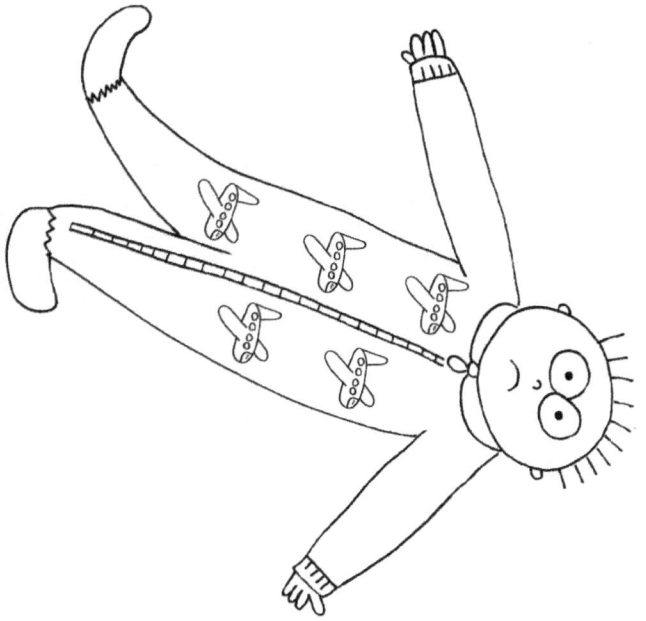

I

bed

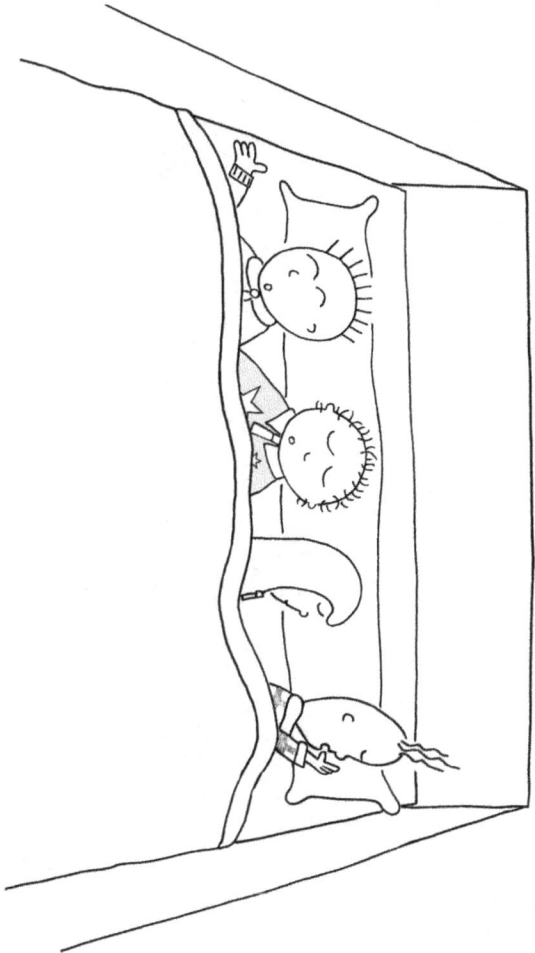

10

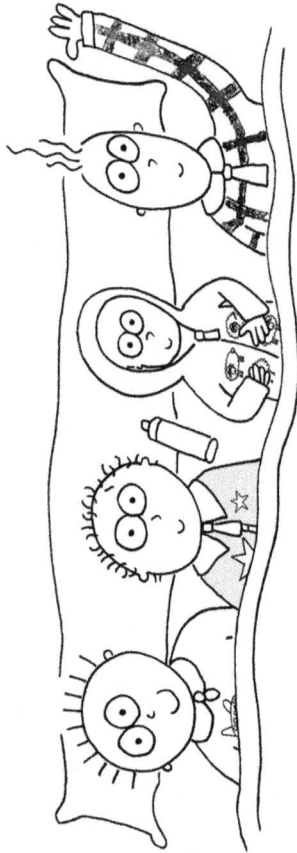

Ned

2

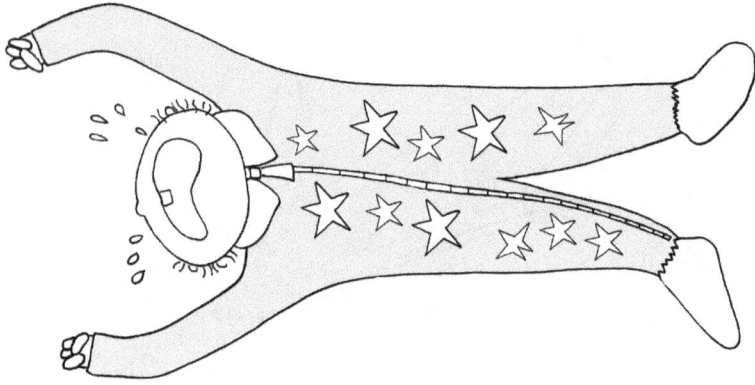

fed

cut

9

3

cut

Ed

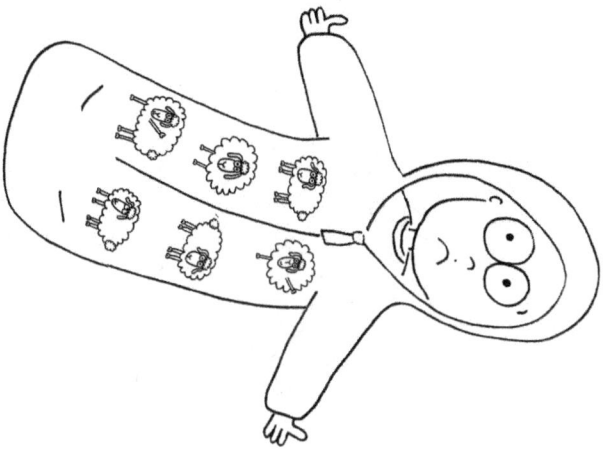

Jed

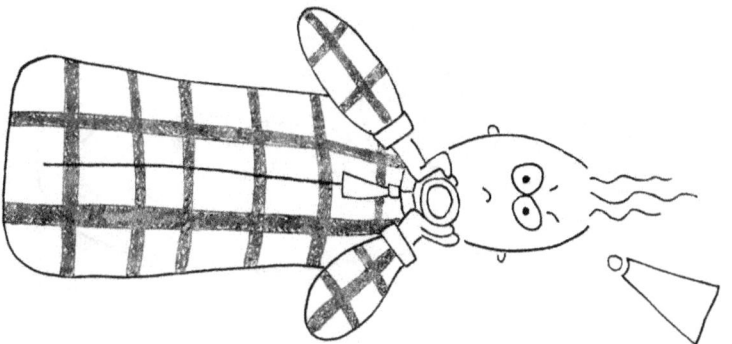

3

8

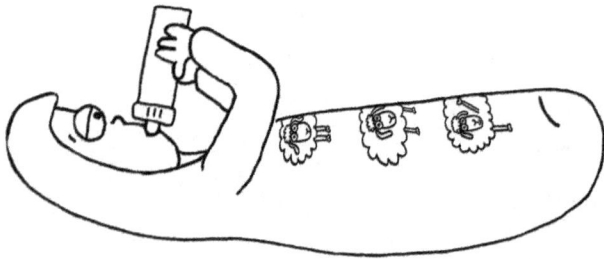

Jed

Ed

SET 1.1 - Book 2 - GUMDROPS FOR MOPPET TOPS

5

cut

Ted

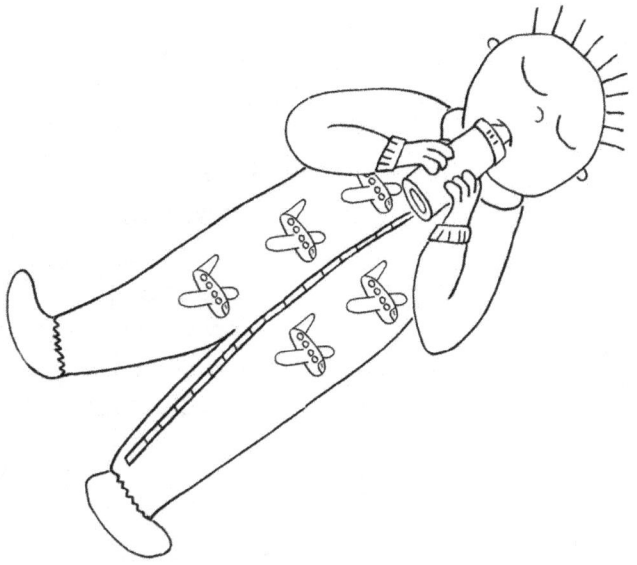

6

Ned

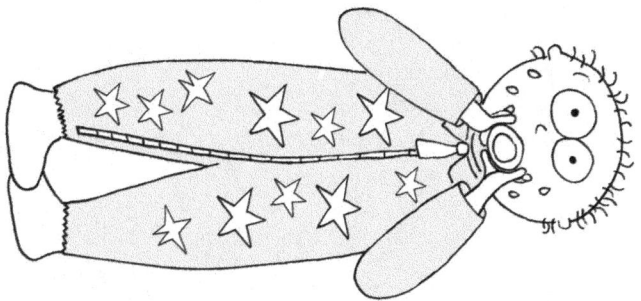

bartlebysbox.com

HIT IT

Story and Pictures by Mark Linley

GUMDROPS for MOPPET TOPS

SET 1.1

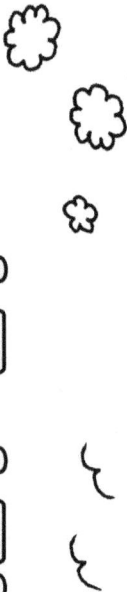

Got it!

HIT IT

sit   hit

bartlebysbox.com

cut

I —

cut

sit

hit

I —

IO

bartlebysbox.com

sit

2

sit

q

cut

SET 1.1 - Book 3 - GUMDROPS FOR MOPPET TOPS

3

cut

sit

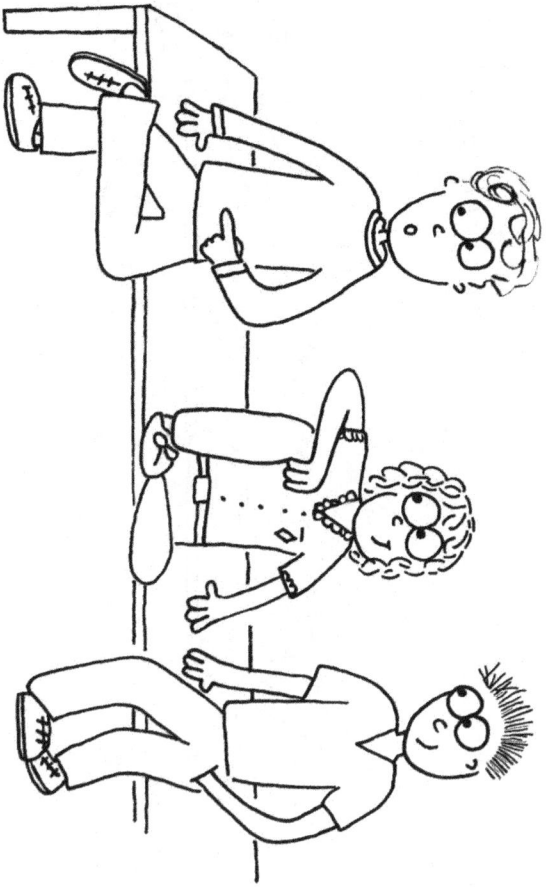

3

hit

8

bartlebysbox.com

sit

hit

7

cut

5

cut

hit

hit

6

bartlebysbox.com

MOM

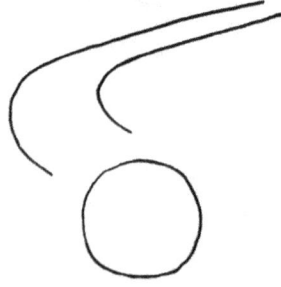

Story and Pictures by Mark Linley

GUMDROPS for MOPPET TOPS

SET 1.1

bartlebysbox.com

cut

Got it!

Mom Tom

MOM

cut

I

Mom

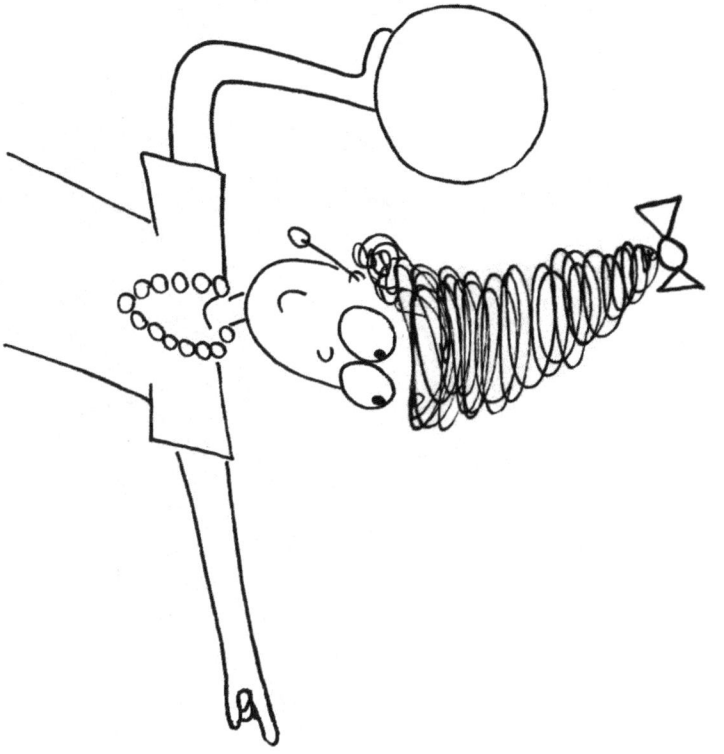

mmmm

10

Tom

2

Tom

Mom

q

cut

3

cut

Mom

Mom

8

Mom

4

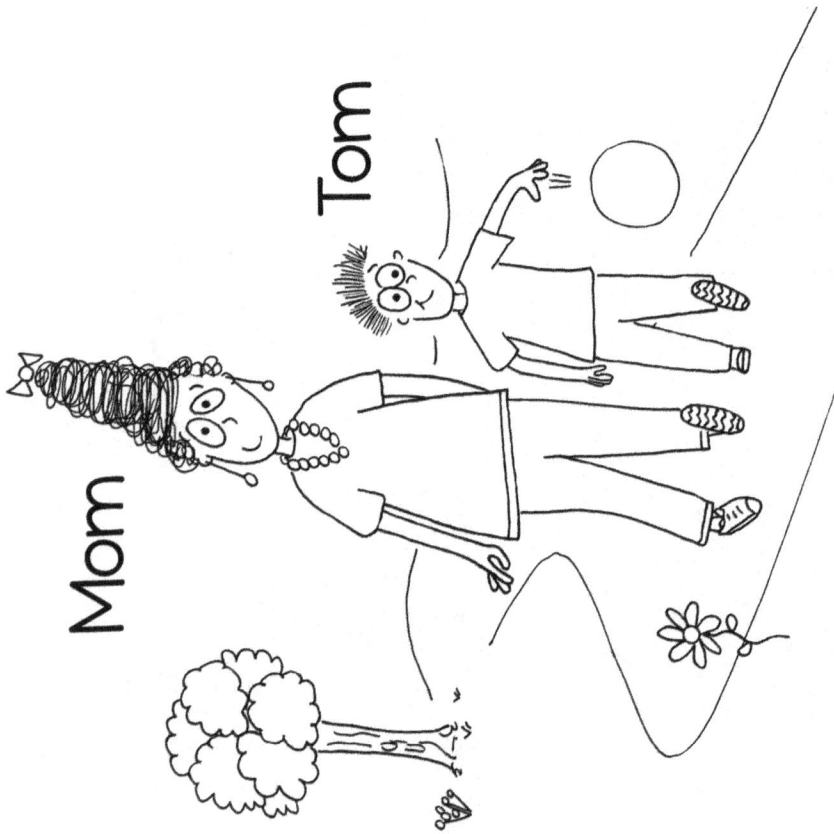

Tom

Mom

7

cut

5

cut

Tom

Tom

6

SUN

SUN

fun run

sun

Got it!

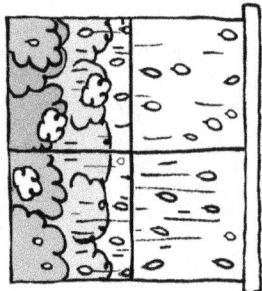

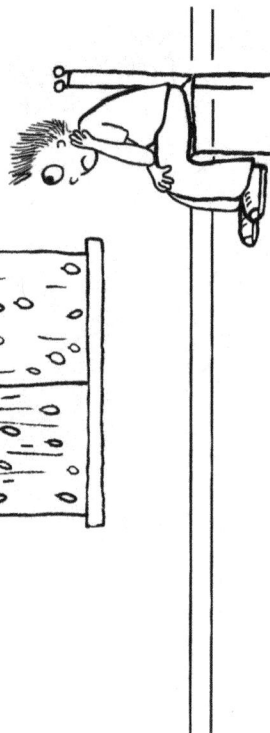

cut

27

cut

1

fun

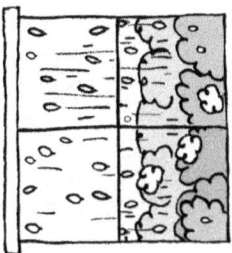

10

fun

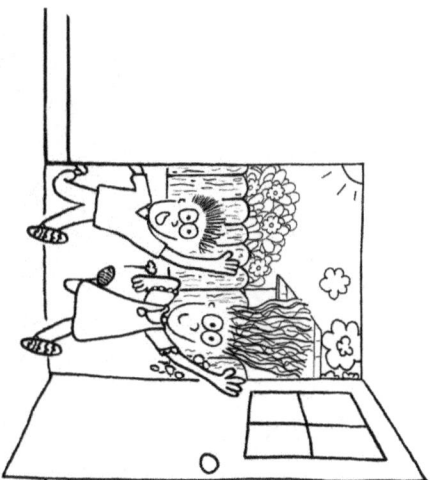
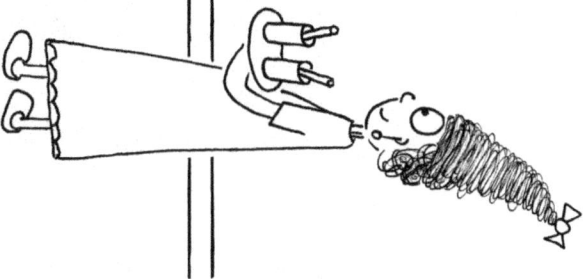

sun

sun

q

cut

SET 1.1 - Book 5 - GUMDROPS FOR MOPPET TOPS

3

cut

sun

8

fun

bartlebysbox.com

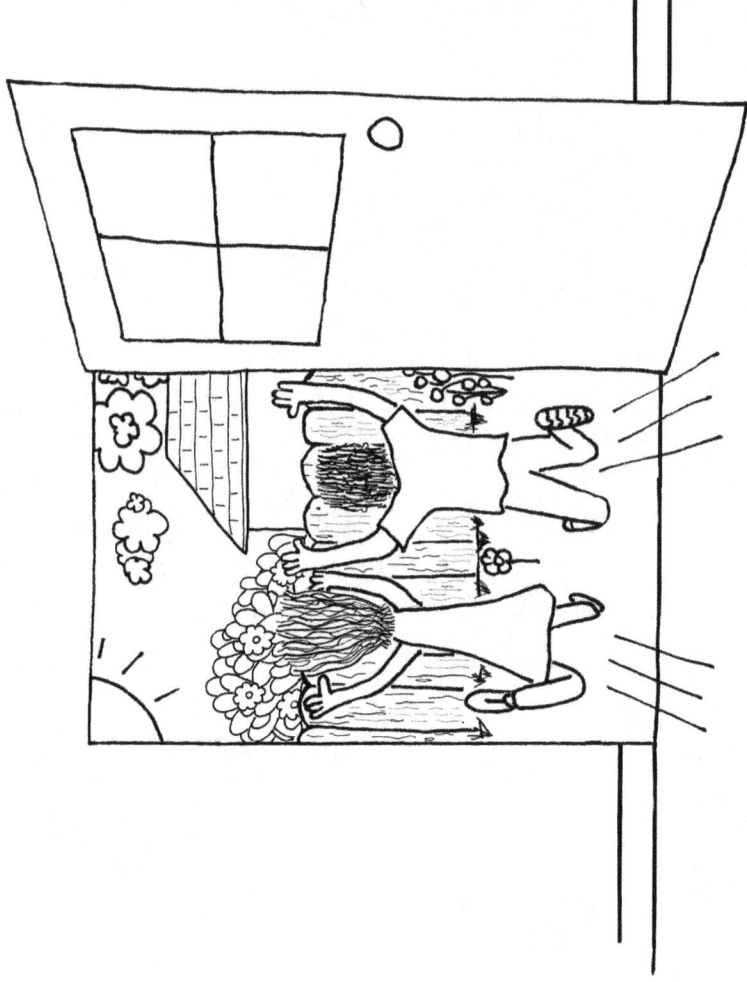

fun

4

fun

7

cut

5

cut

run

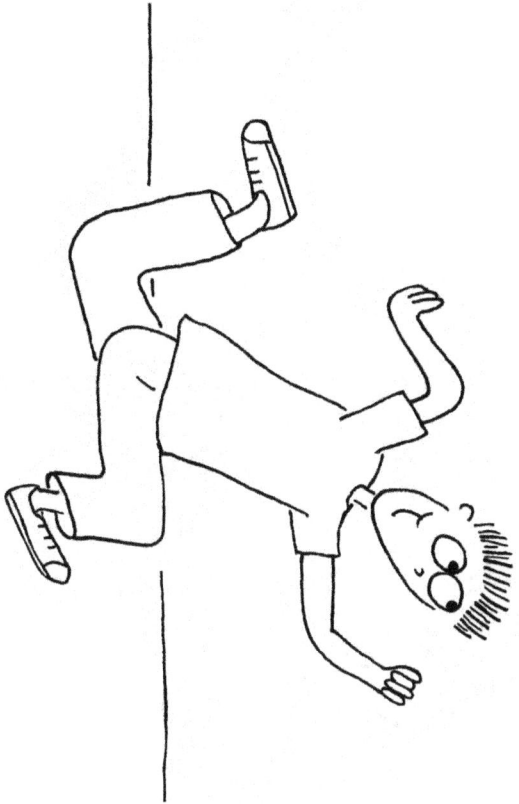

5

6

run

HAT

rat hat
cat mat

Got it!

Story and Pictures by Mark Linley

SET 1.2

GUMDROPS for MOPPET TOPS

Copyright © 2017 by Mark Linley
All Rights Reserved
MADE IN THE USA

HAT

bartlebysbox.com

cut

I

cut

I

rat

rat

10

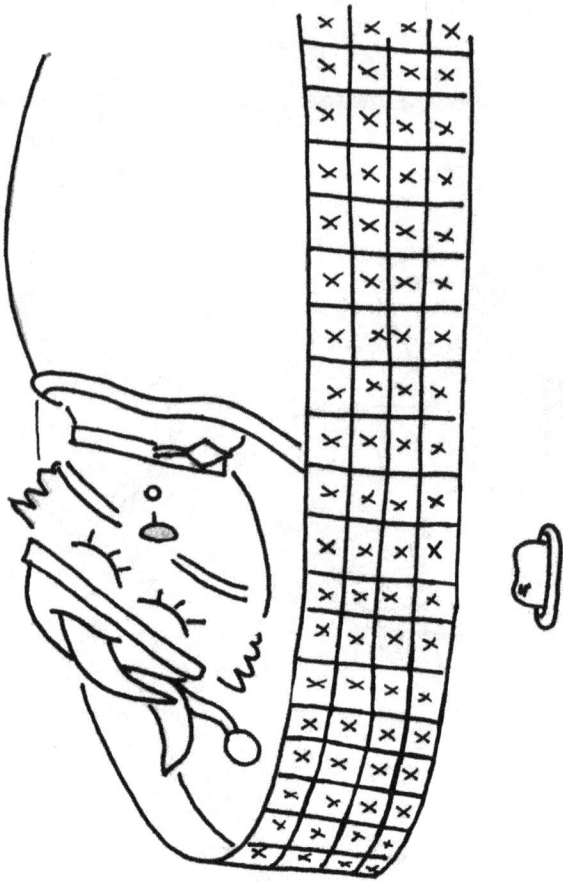

cat

2

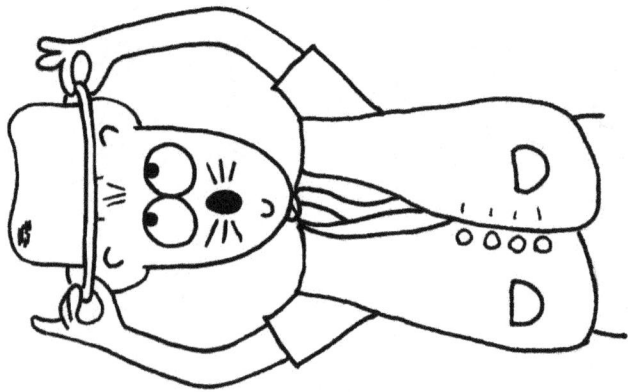

hat

9

SET 1.2 - Book 1 - GUMDROPS FOR MOPPET TOPS

3

cut

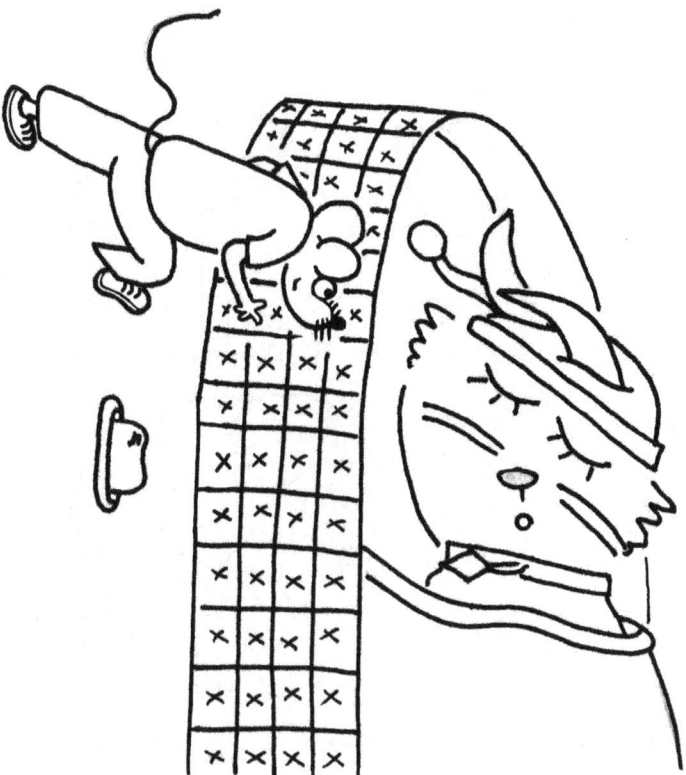

hat

mat

3

8

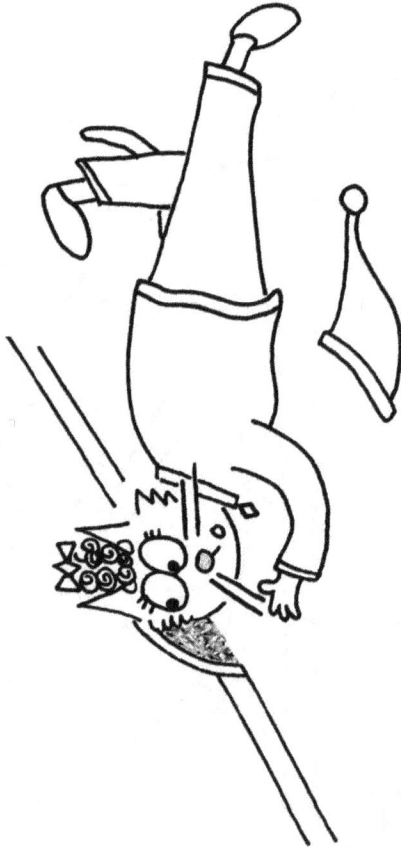

hat

4

7

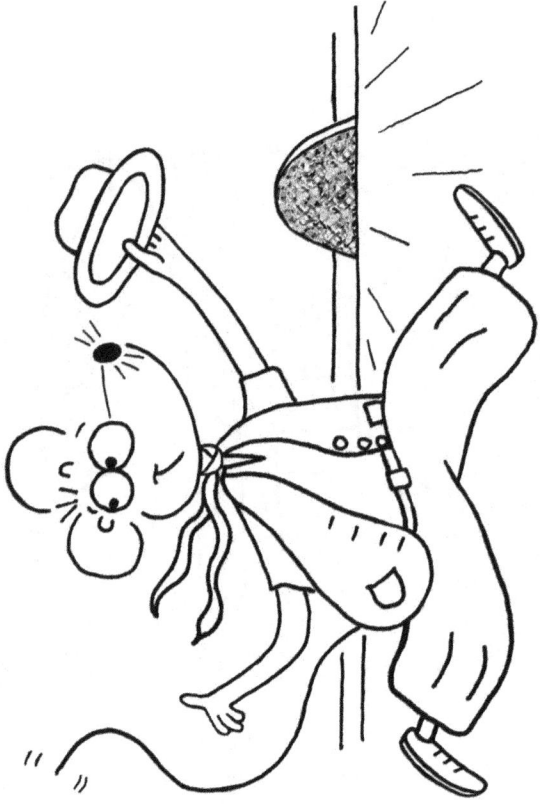

cat

7

cut

SET 1.2 - Book 1 - GUMDROPS FOR MOPPET TOPS

37

cat

hat

5

cut

5

6

WET

Story and Pictures by Mark Linley

SET 1.2

WET

wet
let
set

pet
get
jet
met

Got it!

bartlebysbox.com

cut

cut

1

pet

set

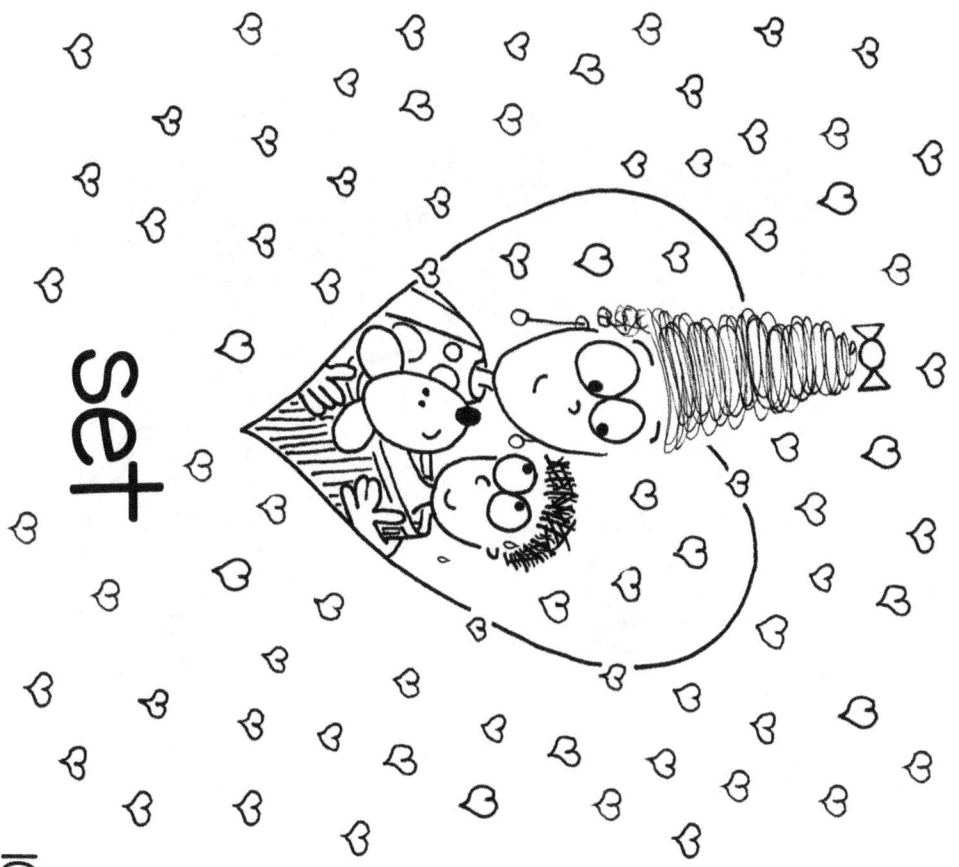

10

get

2

wet

q

SET 1.3 - Book 2 - GUMDROPS FOR MOPPET TOPS

3

cut

pet

let

3

8

jet

4

wet

7

SET 1.2 - Book 2 - GUMDROPS FOR MOPPET TOPS

cut

5

met

6

wet

PIG DIGS

GUMDROPS for MOPPET TOPS

SET 1.2

Story and Pictures by Mark Linley

bartlebysbox.com

cut

PIG DIGS

pig   big
dig   jig
wig

Got it!

cut

I

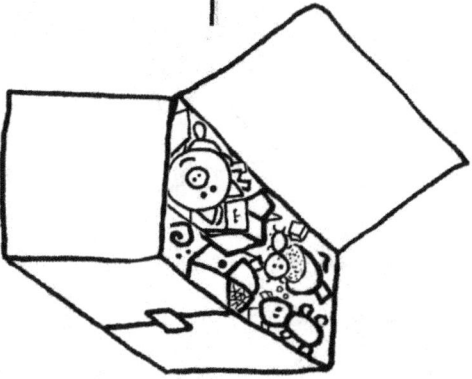

pig

jig

10

dig

2

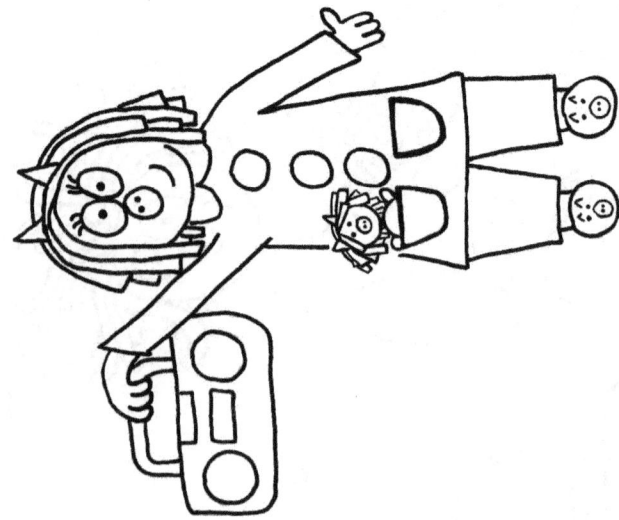

big

q

cut

SET 1.2 - Book 3 - GUMDROPS FOR MOPPET TOPS

3

cut

wig

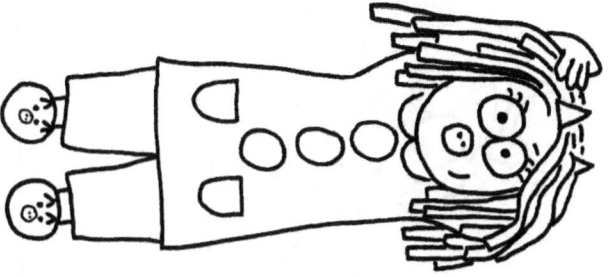

3

8

dig

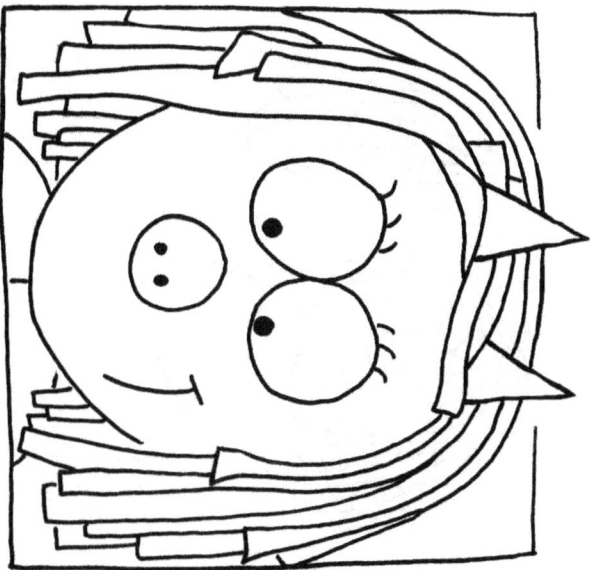

dig

4

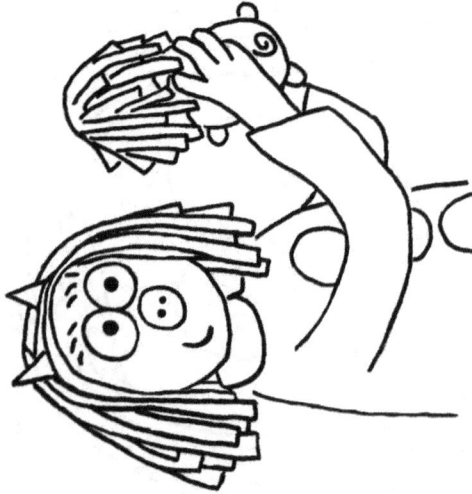

wig

7

SET 1.2 - Book 3 - GUMDROPS FOR MOPPET TOPS

pig

5

cut

dig

6

bartlebysbox.com

DOG JOGS

Story and Pictures by Mark Linley

GUMDROPS for MOPPET TOPS — SET 1.2

DOG JOGS

dog   fog
jog   log

Got it!

bartlebysbox.com

cut

cut

I

dog

jog

10

jog

2

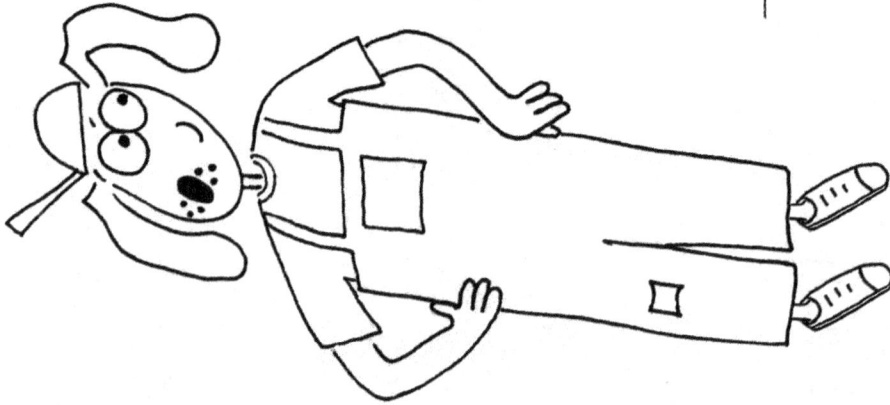

dog

q

cut

SET 1.2 - Book 4 - GUMDROPS FOR MOPPET TOPS

bartlebysbox.com

3

cut

jog

3

log

8

fog

4

log

7

cut

cut

5

fog

6

log

bartlebysbox.com

HUG

Story and Pictures by Mark Linley

SET 1.2

GUMDROPS for MOPPET TOPS

Got it!

hug tug jug
mug

HUG

bartlebysbox.com

cut

57

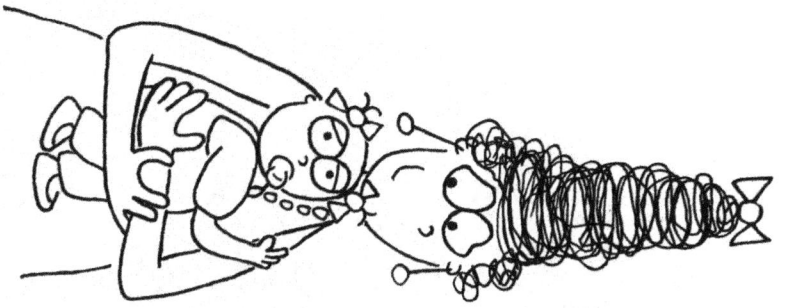

hug

hug

cut

SET 1.2 - Book 5 - GUMDROPS FOR MOPPET TOPS

hug

2

mug

q

cut

3

cut

mug

3

8

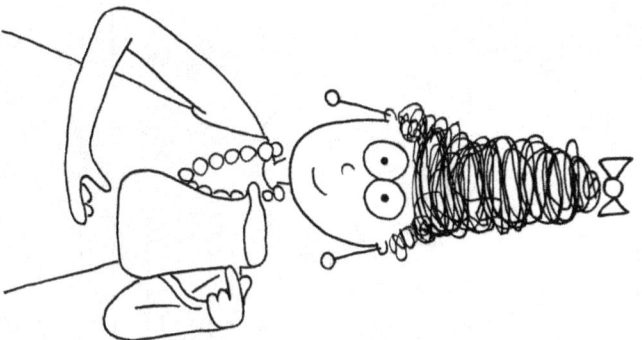

jug

4

mug

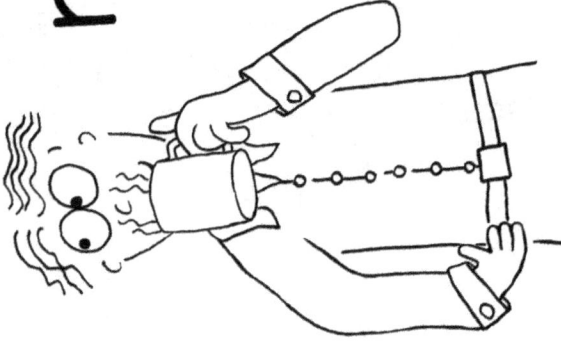

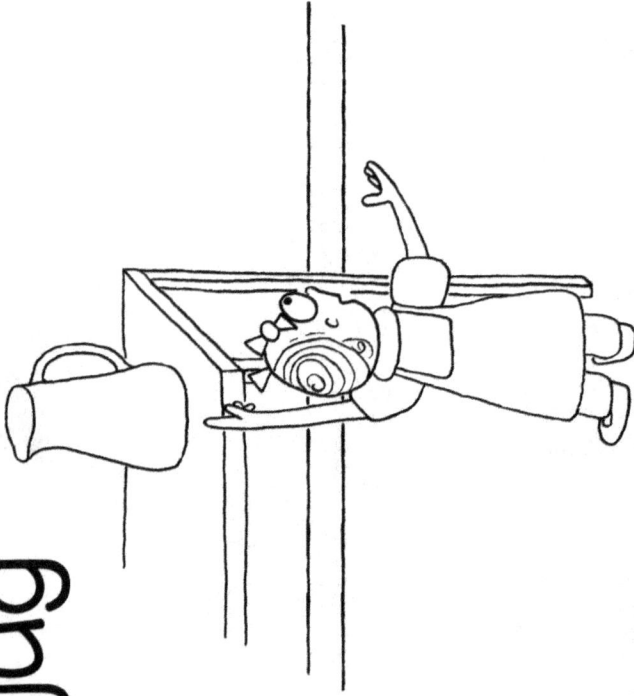

jug

7

5

cut

tug

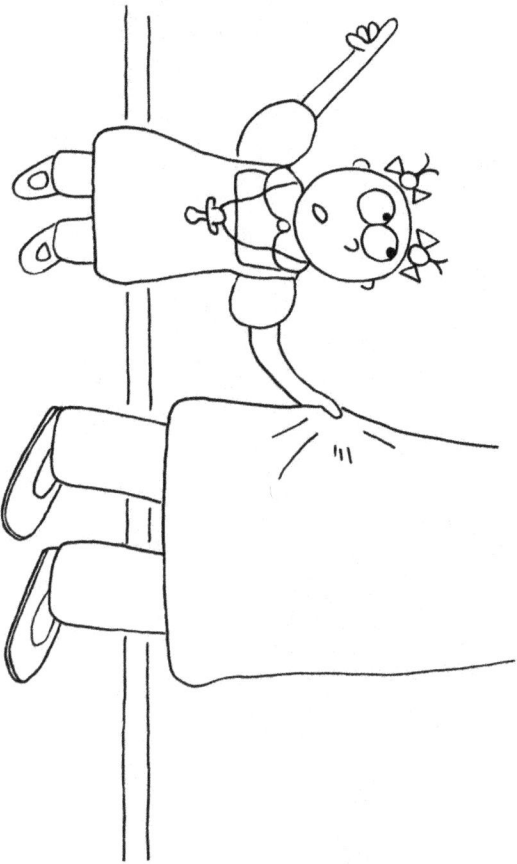

6

tug

FAT RAT

Story and Pictures by Mark Linley

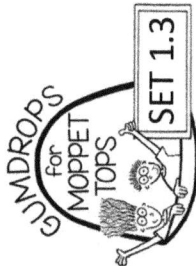

SET 1.3

FAT RAT

hat   cat

rat   fat

Got it!

bartlebysbox.com

cut

1

hat

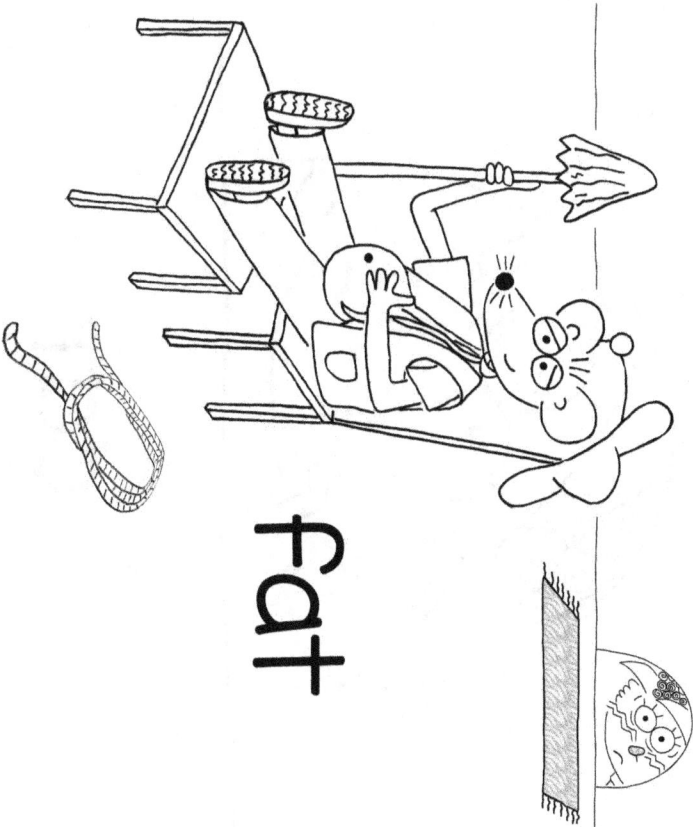

fat

10

rat

2

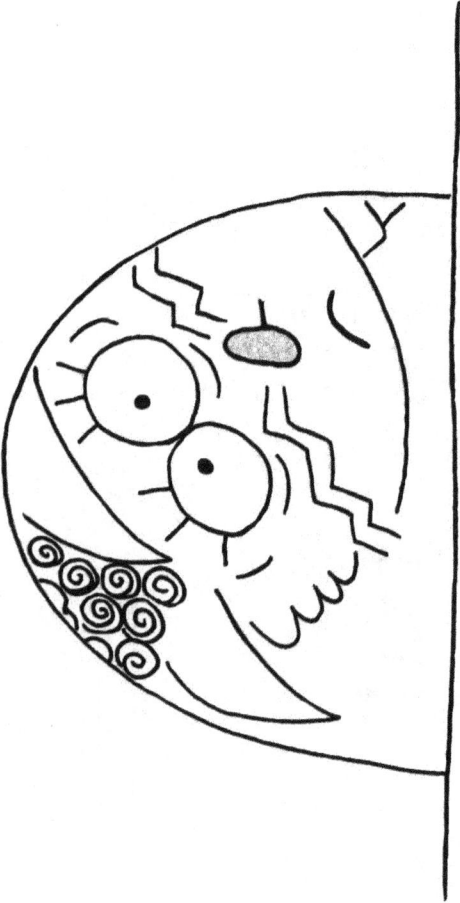

cat

q

cut

q

SET 1.3 - Book 1 - GUMDROPS FOR MOPPET TOPS

3

cut

rat

8

cat

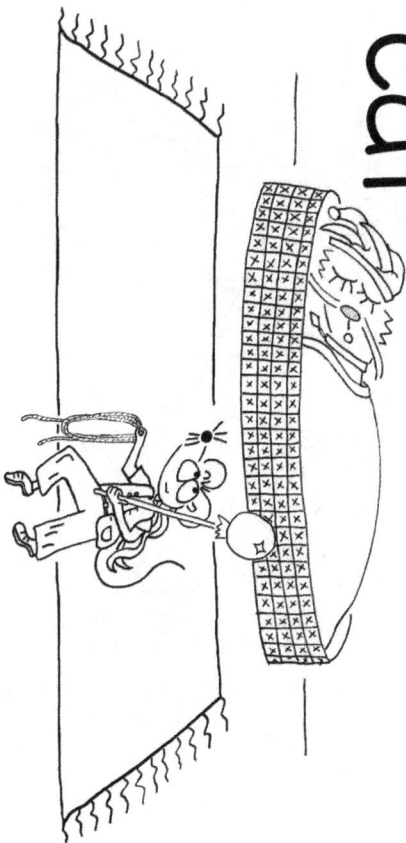

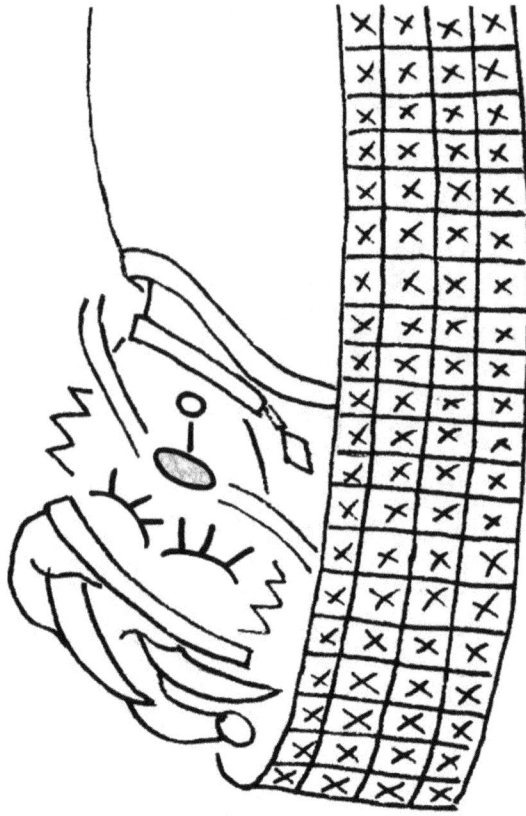

cat

4

7

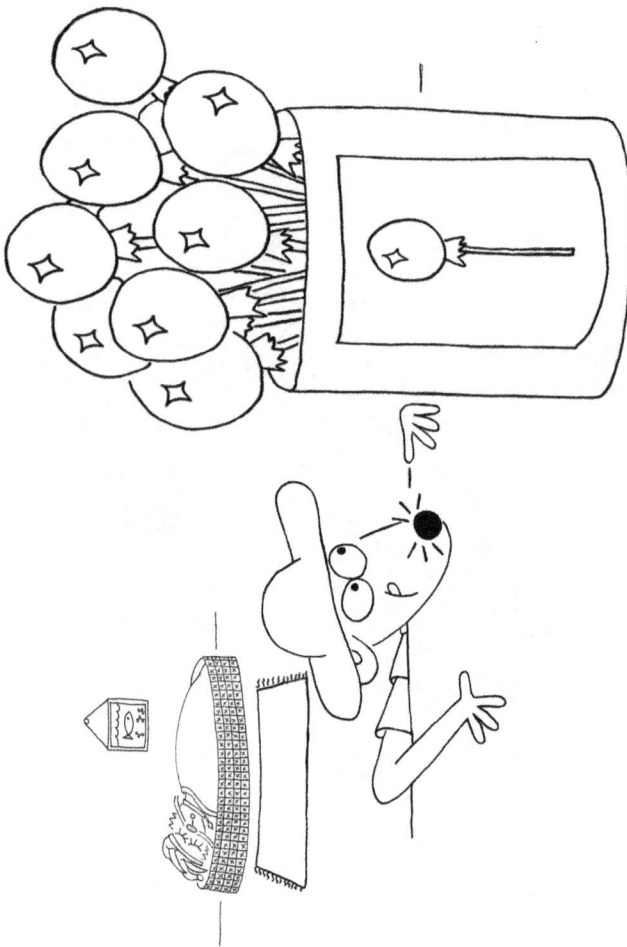

mmmm

cut

—

5

cut

cat

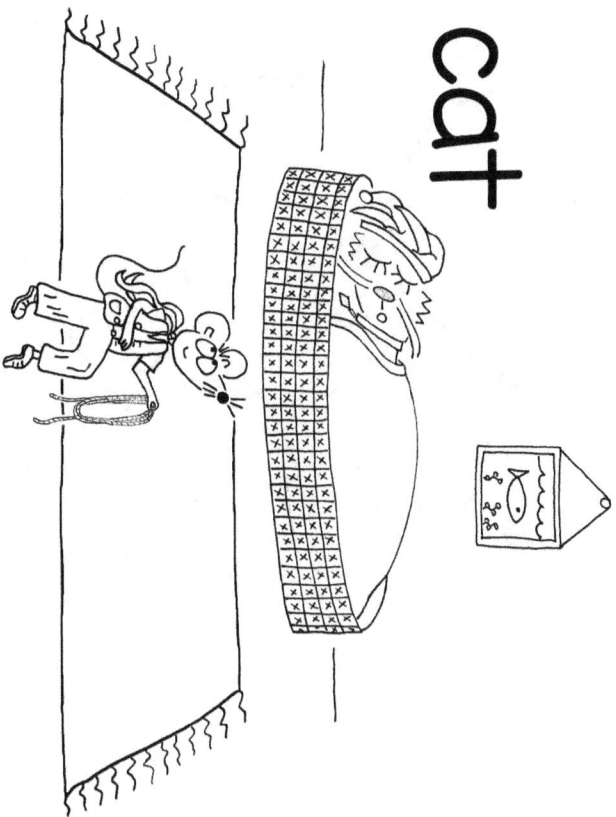

rat

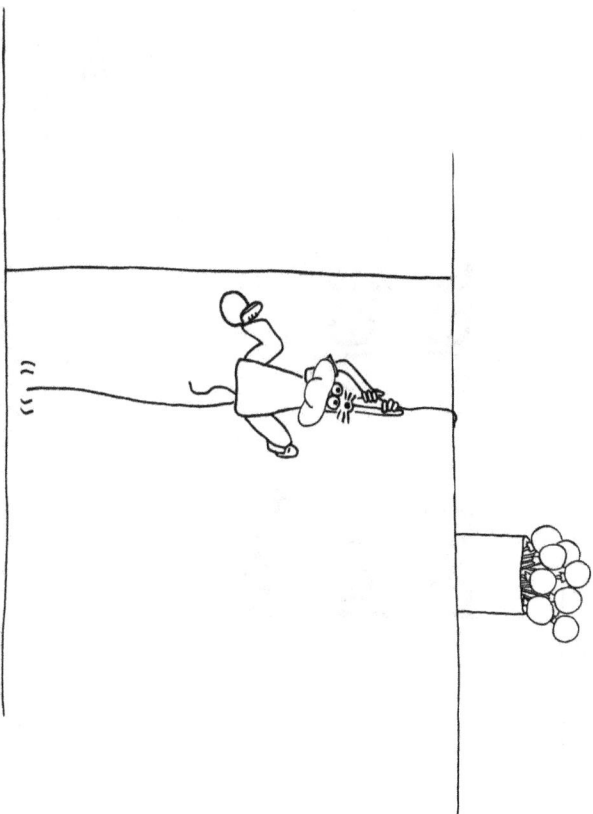

6

WET PET

Story and Pictures by Mark Linley

GUMDROPS for MOPPET TOPS

SET 1.3

WET PET

pet net

let get

wet

Got it!

bartlebysbox.com

cut

cut

pet

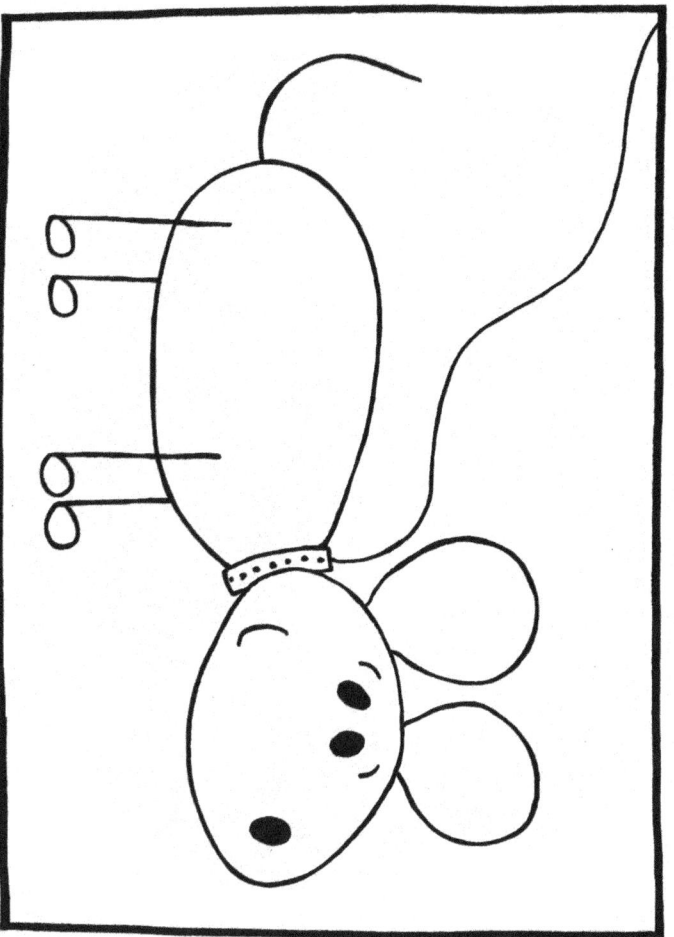

pet

pet

2

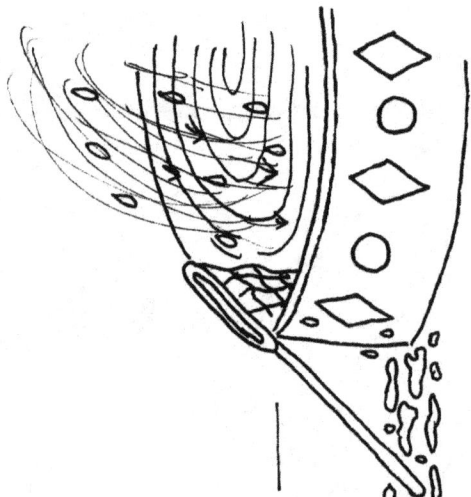

get

q

SET 1.3 - Book 2 - GUMDROPS FOR MOPPET TOPS

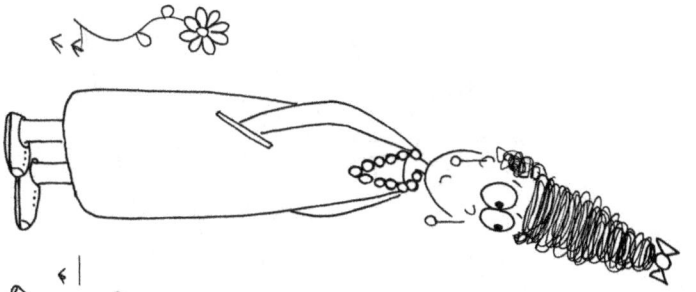

3

cut

let

net

8

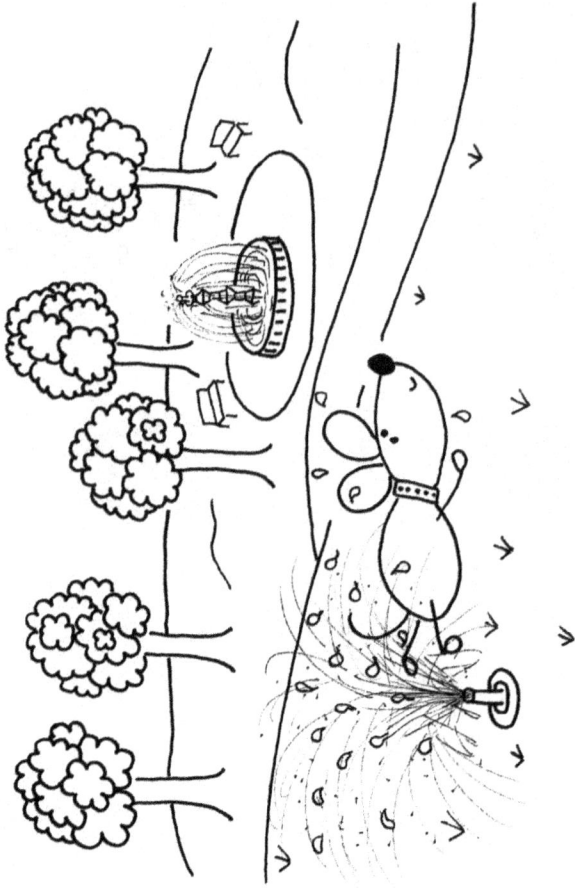

wet

bartlebysbox.com

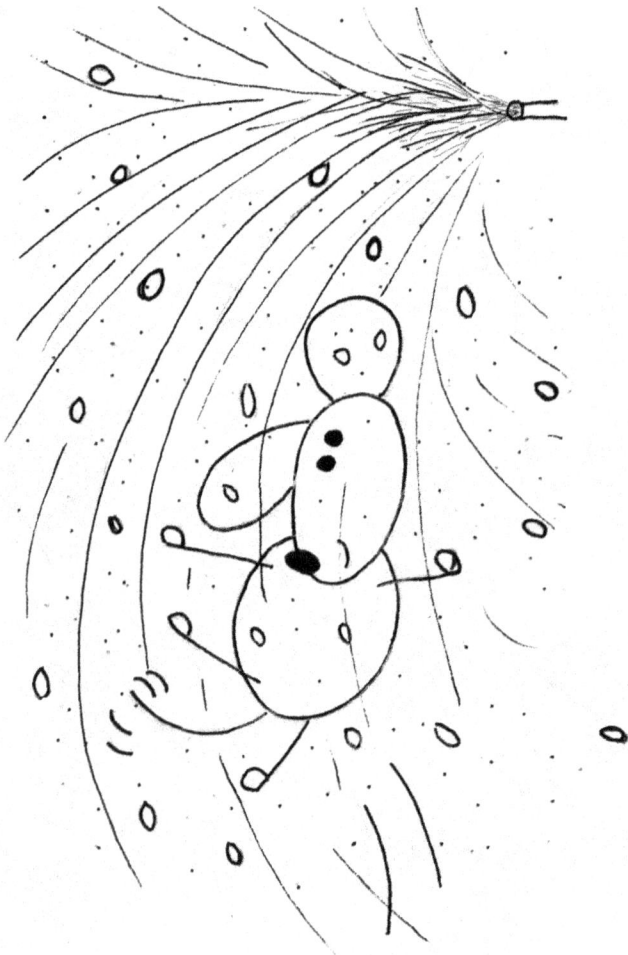

wet

cut

SET 1.3 - Book 2 - GUMDROPS FOR MOPPET TOPS

5

cut

wet

6

wet

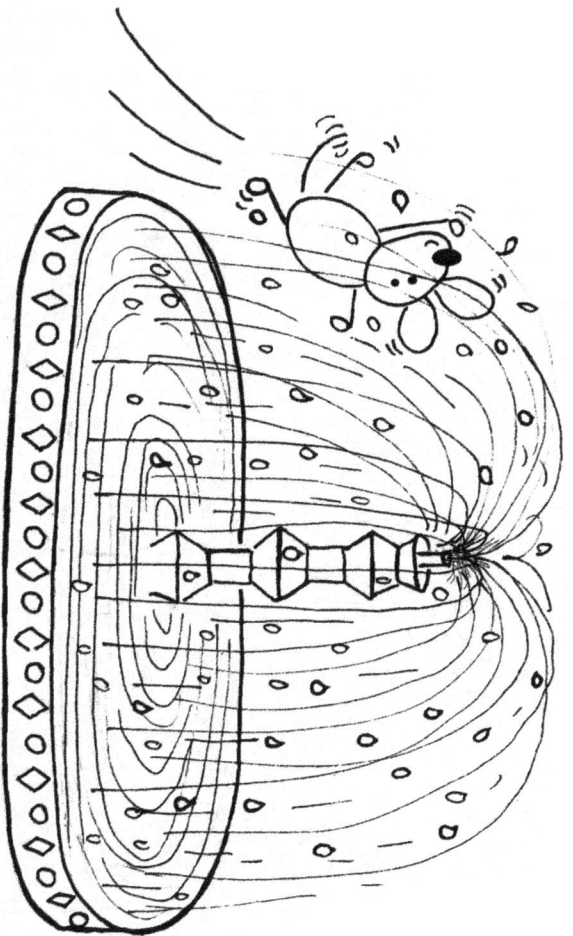

BIG DIG

Story and Pictures by Mark Linley

GUMDROPS for MOPPET TOPS

SET 1.3

bartlebysbox.com

cut

BIG DIG

pig

wig

dig

big

Got it!

cut

1

pig

wig

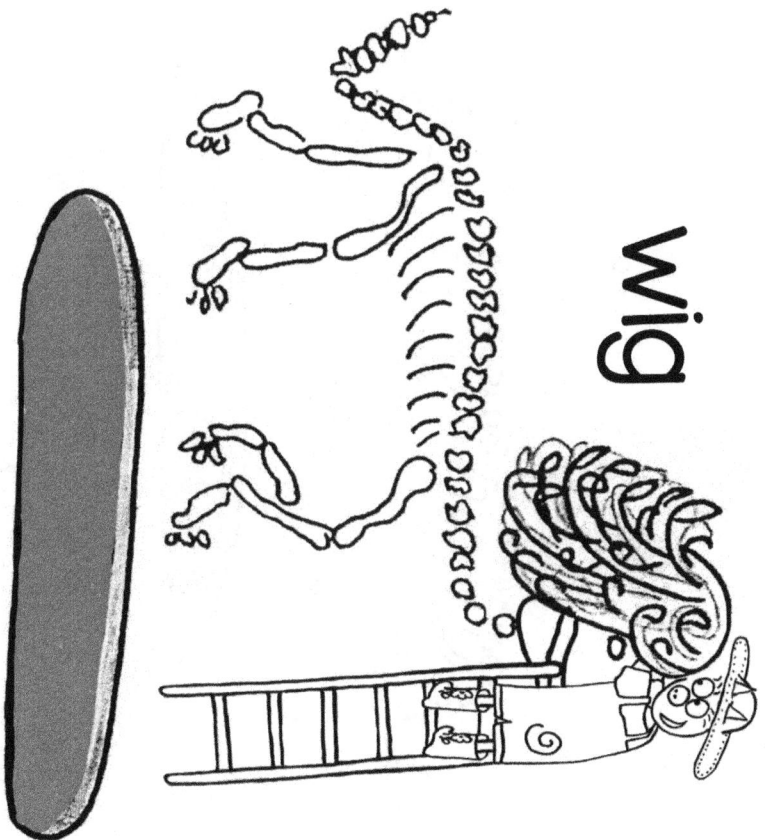

10

wig

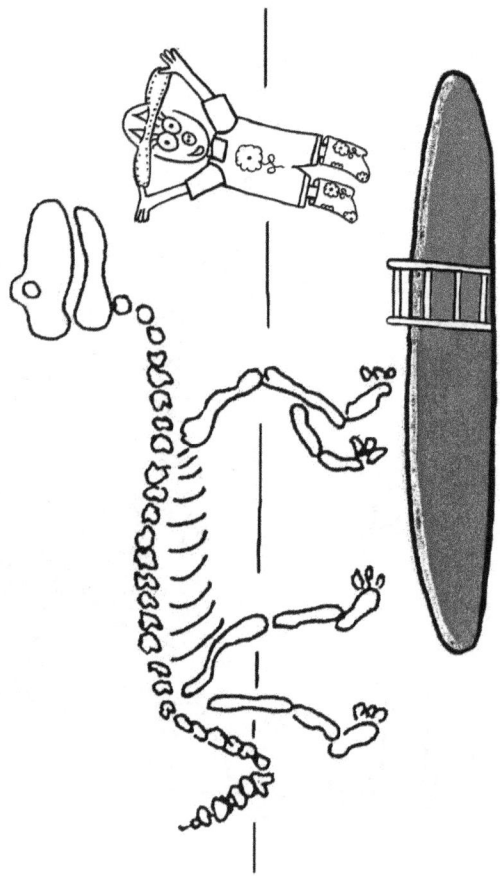

big

3

cut

dig

3

8

big

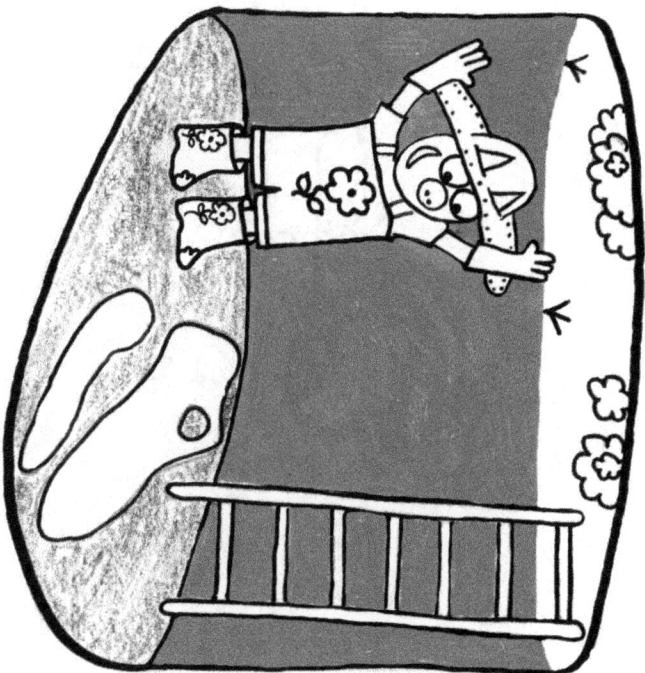

big

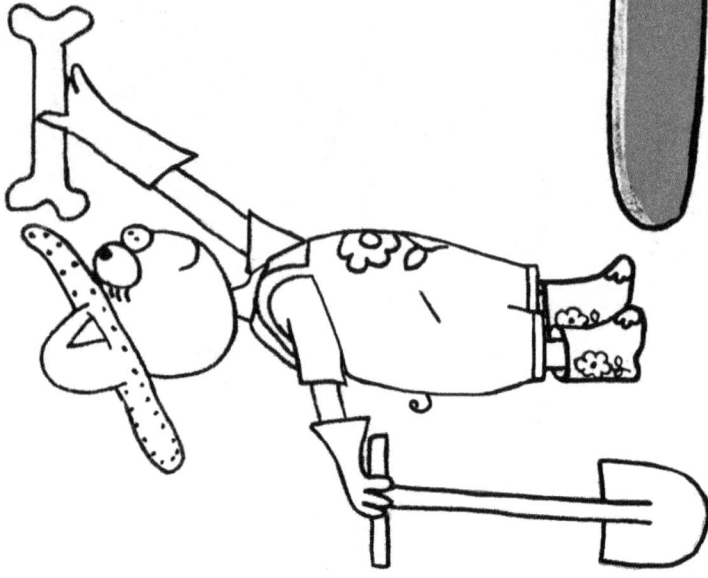

4

dig

7

cut

5

cut

dig

cut

6

big

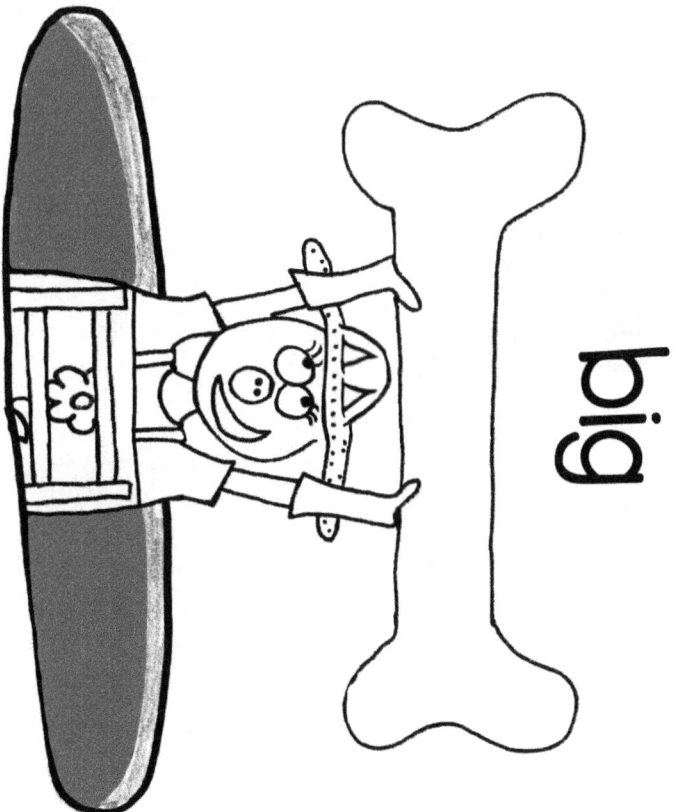

HOP

Story and Pictures by Mark Linley

GUMDROPS for MOPPET TOPS **SET 1.3**

Got it!

pop
mop

hop
top
cop

HOP

bartlebysbox.com

cut

cut

I _____ hop _____

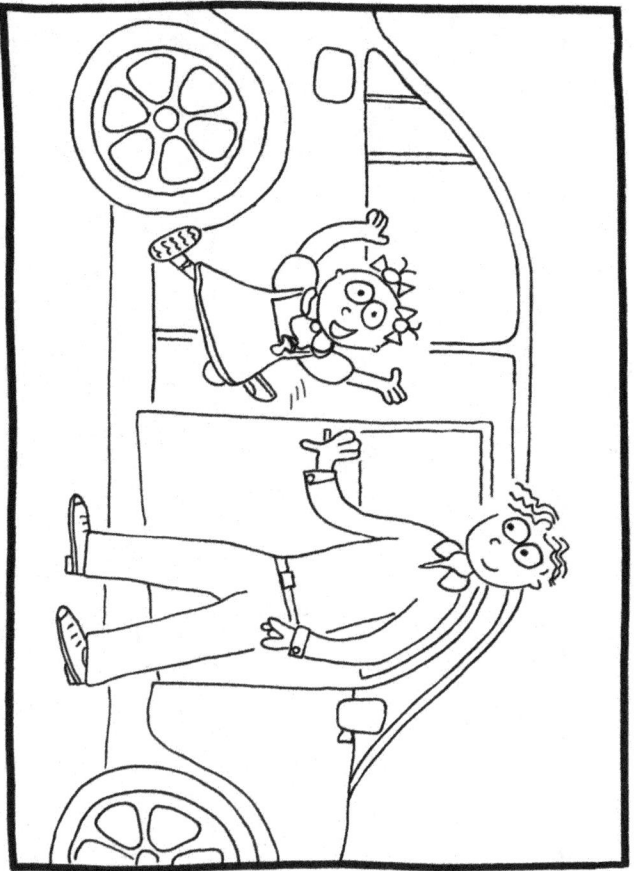

I _____ mop _____ 10

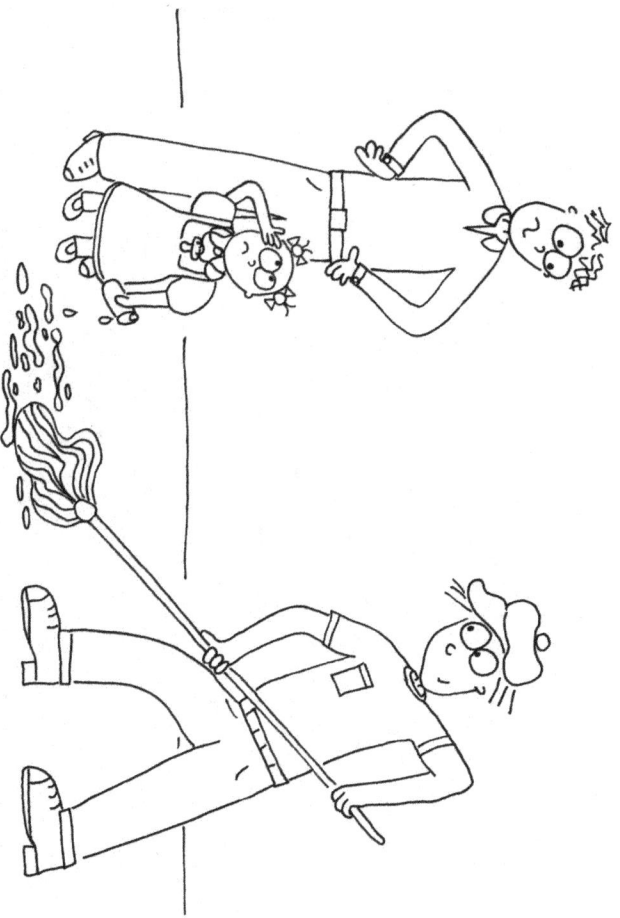

hop

2

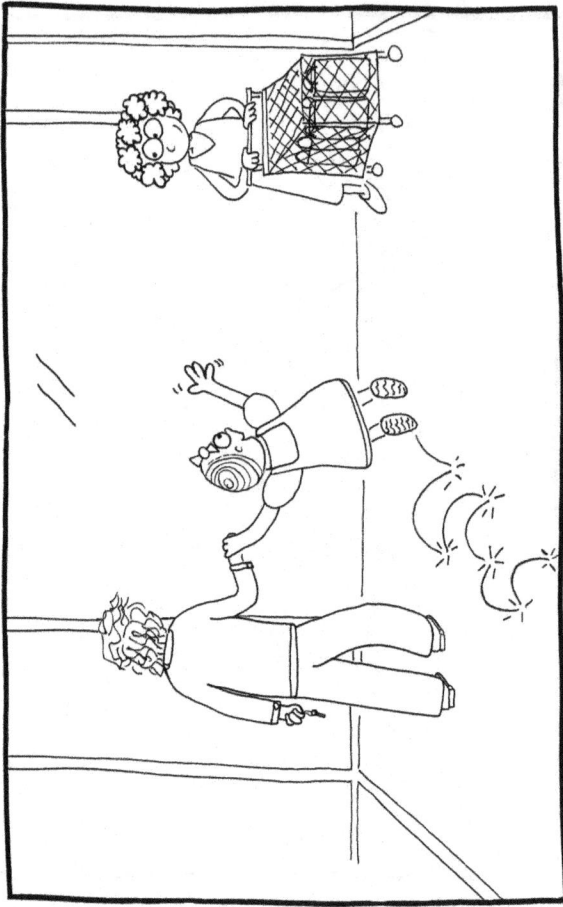

pop

q

cut

SET 1.3 - Book 4 - GUMDROPS FOR MOPPET TOPS

3

cut

hop

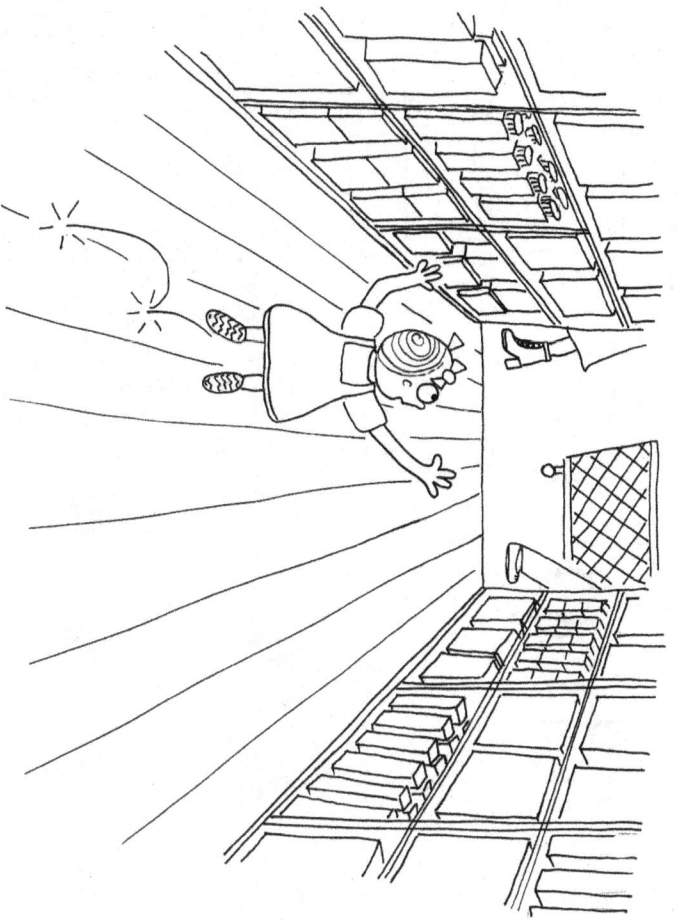

hop

8

bartlebysbox.com

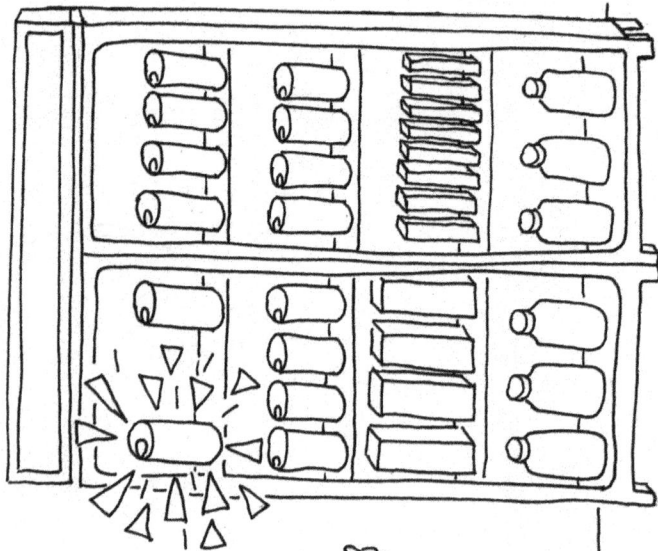

top

4

hop

7

bartlebysbox.com

cut

5

cut

hop

6

cop

GUM

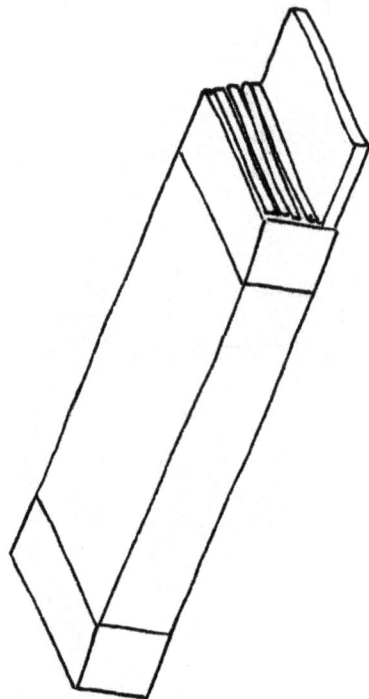

GUM

gum hum
yum

Got it!

GUMDROPS for MOPPET TOPS SET 1.3

bartlebysbox.com

cut

87

cut

I

bartsbysbox.com

10

yum

hum

2

q

cut

89

bartlebysbox.com

3

cut

yum

yum

8

hum

gum

cut

SET 1.3 - Book 5 - GUMDROPS FOR MOPPET TOPS

5

gum

5

6

yum

bartlebysbox.com

LESSON PLANS

Sequence of Instruction

Provided here is a suggested Lesson Plan for teaching CVC decoding in tandem with reading comprehension.

OPENING QUESTIONS

Ask one or more questions from **BEFORE READING** (See **Comprehension Questions**, following)

INTRODUCE the CVC WORDS

PREVIEW the book's CVC words on the board (Use the Back Cover of the book for a list of words)

> *Procedure for Demonstrating Blending, Sound by Sound*
> 1. Write one CVC word from the book on the board
>   Point to each letter and enunciate the sound of each letter: /c/ - /a/ - /t/
>   Point to the first two letters and enunciate the first two phonemes, then
>   the final consonant: /ca/ - /t/. Or, point to the first letter and
>   enunciate the first phoneme, then the medial vowel and final consonant:
>   /c/ - /at/
>   Swipe your finger under the word and blend the entire word: 'cat'
> 2. Repeat the above sequence as your students chorally read along with you
> 3. Write the next word, and so on....

READ TOGETHER

GIVE students their own copies of the book
READ each page

> For each page, consider doing the following:
> 1. ENCOURAGE students to look at the picture and make comments
> 2. ASK questions from **DURING READING** (See **Comprehension Questions**, following)
> 3. DECODE the page's word
>   Teacher: *Put your finger under the first letter. Ready begin.*
>   Teacher and students: /c/ - /a/ - /t/, /ca/ - /t/
>   or /c/ - /a/ - /t/, /c/ - /at/
>   Teacher: *What's the word?*
>   Teacher and students: *'cat'*

CONTINUE reading the entire book

CLOSING

DIRECT students to read the words on the Back Cover independently
ASK questions from **AFTER READING** (See **Comprehension Questions**, following)
ASSIGN further study
    Students re-read the book
    Students retell the story to a friend
    Students follow up with GUMDROPS for MOPPET TOPS Independent Practice Worksheets
    Students spell the words with their own letter cards (sets of letters can be made with
        marker on index cards)
    Students write the words
    Students color the books
    Students take the books home to read with family

Comprehension Questions

Provided here are a variety of questions to ask your students BEFORE, DURING, and AFTER they read. Some teachers may ask many or all of the questions, some teachers only a few. Often one question alone will yeild a rich and lengthy discussion. Many of these questions can be used as writing prompts as well. Of course, a teacher may decide to ask no comprehension questions at all, making their lesson a strictly phonics one.

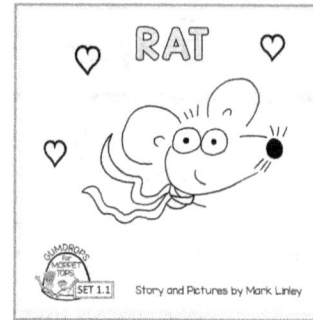

RAT

BEFORE READING

Do you have a piece of clothing that you especially like? What is it? Why is it special to you?

Do you ever wear a hat? Does anyone you know ever wear a hat? What kind of hat?

What kinds of hats do people wear?

(Some possible responses: Hard hats, sun hats, rain hats, helmets, baseball hats, uniform hats, hoods, winter hats, swimming caps, fancy hats, straw hats, cowboy hats, ski caps, beanies, bucket hats...)

Why do people wear hats? (For sun, shade, protection, rain, fashion…)

DURING READING

Title Page	Do you think Rat is friendly? What in the picture makes you think this?
Page 1	What does this picture make you think about? If Rat could speak to you, what might he say? What would you say to him?
Page 2	What is this a picture of? What kind of hat is this? (a bowler) What is this kind of hat used for? (dressing up)
Page 3	What is happening in this picture?
Page 4	Why is Rat jumping? How does he feel? What is he happy about?
Page 5	Why is Rat so excited about his hat? Have you ever been happy about something you wear? A new jacket? A new pair of shoes? What is it? Why does it make you happy?
Page 6	What is going on here? What do you think of what Rat is doing?
Page 7	What is Rat doing with his hat?
Page 8	Is Rat trying to tell us something about his hat?
Page 9	Who is this? Do you think Rat likes Cat? What does Cat want? How does Rat feel when he sees Cat?
Page 10	What happened to Rat? Why did Rat leave? Why does Cat want Rat's hat? Have you ever had something taken from you? What was it? What happened?

AFTER READING

What were you thinking about as you read this book?

How did Rat's feelings change in this book?

If you were a rat, or a small animal, would you like cats? Why or why not?

What might happen next in the story?

Comprehension Questions

Provided here are a variety of questions to ask your students BEFORE, DURING, and AFTER they read. Some teachers may ask many or all of the questions, some teachers only a few. Often one question alone will yeild a rich and lengthy discussion. Many of these questions can be used as writing prompts as well. Of course, a teacher may decide to ask no comprehension questions at all, making their lesson a strictly phonics one.

SET 1.1 - Book 2

FED

BEFORE READING

Have you ever been around a baby? Who was it?

What are twins? Triplets? Quadruplets?

Why do babies cry? (Hunger, needs a diaper change, sleepy, teething, tummy aches. gas, fever, too hot or cold, needs to burp, wants to be held)

Have you ever helped to take care of a baby? What did you do?

DURING READING

Title Page	What is this? What is in it? Why are baby bottles used?
Page 1	How is Ted feeling? How do you know from the picture that Ted feels this way?
Page 2	How is Ned feeling?
Page 3	How is Ed feeling?
Page 4	How is Jed feeling? What do the boys want? What do babies want? Why are the boys so upset?
Page 5	How does Ted feel now? What is he thinking? What in the picture makes you think this?
Page 6	How does Ned feel now?
Page 7	How does Ed feel now?
Page 8	How does Jed feel now?
Page 9	What is happening here?
Page 10	What happened? Do you feel sleepy after you eat?

AFTER READING

How did the boys' feelings change in this book?

What was the problem? How was it solved?

Do you have baby brothers or sisters or cousins? What are they like?

What has to be done to take care of them?

Do you have any stories about when you were a baby? What are they?

Comprehension Questions

Provided here are a variety of questions to ask your students BEFORE, DURING, and AFTER they read. Some teachers may ask many or all of the questions, some teachers only a few. Often one question alone will yeild a rich and lengthy discussion. Many of these questions can be used as writing prompts as well. Of course, a teacher may decide to ask no comprehension questions at all, making their lesson a strictly phonics one.

HIT IT

BEFORE READING

What sports do you like to play?
What sport do you most want to learn to play?
Do you play handball?
What are the rules of handball?

DURING READING

Title Page   What is this a picture of? What game is shown here?

Page 1   What is the boy doing?

Page 2   What are the kids looking at?

Page 3   What are the kids doing? Are they waiting for something? Are you able to wait your turn, or do you get upset if you have to wait? Do you ever cut in line?

Page 4   What are the kids watching? What might the girl be thinking?

Page 5   What is happening here?

Page 6   Who hits the ball harder? Who do you think will win? Why do you think that? Is there enough in the picture to tell who will win?

Page 7   Is hitting the ball hard the only way to win at handball? Are there other ways to play the game that could help to win the game?

Page 8   What happened to the boy? Do you think the boy is hurt? How so?

Page 9   The boy who lost the game to the girl is now sitting on the bench. Why does the boy look like this? How is he feeling? What is his friend saying to him? How does the girl feel?

Page 10   What is the girl thinking about now?

AFTER READING

How much time passes in this story?
Do you like to win when you are playing a game? How important is winning to you? How does it feel to win?
What thoughts do you have when you win?
How does it feel to lose? Is it okay to lose? What does it mean to be a bad sport?
If someone feels bad or sad, what can you do to make him or her feel better? What can you say?
Why is it important to do you best?
Is there a lesson or moral to be learned from this story?

Comprehension Questions

Provided here are a variety of questions to ask your students BEFORE, DURING, and AFTER they read. Some teachers may ask many or all of the questions, some teachers only a few. Often one question alone will yeild a rich and lengthy discussion. Many of these questions can be used as writing prompts as well. Of course, a teacher may decide to ask no comprehension questions at all, making their lesson a strictly phonics one.

SET 1.1 - Book 4

MOM

BEFORE READING

Do you like to play ball games?

What ball games do you like to play?

Do you play ball games with your parents or other family members? What do you play?

Do you know the game of 'catch'? Are there rules to the game of 'catch'? How is it played? What does a player try to do while playing 'catch'?

DURING READING

Title Page	Do you like to play catch? Who do you play with? Where do you play catch?
Page 1	What is happening here? Are you good at throwing balls? Are big balls or small balls easier to throw? How are balls different from one another? (weight, size, bounce, sometimes shape)
Page 2	What is the boy thinking?
Page 3	What happened? Are you good at catching balls?
Page 4	What is the mom doing here? Do you like to kick balls?
Page 5	What is happening here?
Page 6	What did the boy do? What is the boy thinking?
Page 7	What is happening now?
Page 8	How do you feel when your mom or dad gives you something to eat or drink?
Page 9	How does Mom feel about her son? Why do you think this? What is the mom thinking?
Page 10	How does the boy feel about his mom? How can you tell? What is the boy thinking?

AFTER READING

What did you think about as you read this book?

What kind of a person is Mom? What page or pages in the book lead you to think that?

Do you play with your parents? What games do you like to play? What activities do you like to do together?

Why is it important that parents spend time and play with their kids?

Comprehension Questions

Provided here are a variety of questions to ask your students BEFORE, DURING, and AFTER they read. Some teachers may ask many or all of the questions, some teachers only a few. Often one question alone will yeild a rich and lengthy discussion. Many of these questions can be used as writing prompts as well. Of course, a teacher may decide to ask no comprehension questions at all, making their lesson a strictly phonics one.

SUN

BEFORE READING

    Do you like rainy days?
    What do you like about rainy days? What do you dislike about rainy days?
    Do you stay inside on rainy days? What do you play? What do you do?
    Do people in your family like rainy days?
    How is rain good for the Earth? Is rain ever dangerous?

DURING READING

Title Page	Is there a problem here? What is the boy thinking about? How is he feeling? Does the boy feel bored? Do you ever get bored? Are there people who are never bored? What is their secret?
Page 1	What is the girl doing? How is she feeling about the rainy day? What is the boy doing? How is the boy feeling about the rainy day? What do you think he would rather be doing?
Page 2	Look at the window. What is happening outside? How does the boy feel now?
Page 3	How does the boy feel now? What is he saying? What does the girl think?
Page 4	What is happening here?
Page 5	What are the boy and girl doing?
Page 6	How do the kids feel now?
Page 7	If you could talk to the boy or girl, what would you say? What might they say to you?
Page 8	Have you ever been on a teeter-totter (or see-saw)? How does a teeter-totter work?
Page 9	How do the kids feel? Why do they feel this way?
Page 10	What is happening here?

AFTER READING

    What was the problem in this story? How was it solved?
    Do you prefer sun or rain? Why?
    Do you ever like to go out in the rain? What do you do? Do you ever play in the rain?
    What do you do at home on days when you have to stay inside?
    How did the two kids play together? Did they get along? What parts of the story show that they get along?

Comprehension Questions

Provided here are a variety of questions to ask your students BEFORE, DURING, and AFTER they read. Some teachers may ask many or all of the questions, some teachers only a few. Often one question alone will yeild a rich and lengthy discussion. Many of these questions can be used as writing prompts as well. Of course, a teacher may decide to ask no comprehension questions at all, making their lesson a strictly phonics one.

HAT

BEFORE READING

Why do people wear hats? What kinds of hats do people wear? (Some possible responses: Hard hats, sun hats, rain hats, helmets, baseball hats, uniform hats, hoods, winter hats, swimming caps, fancy hats, straw hats, cowboy hats, ski caps, beanies, bucket hast...)

Do you wear a hat? What kind of hat do you wear?

If you could have any kind of hat you wanted, what would it be? Why?

DURING READING

Title Page	What is Rat doing with his hat? Is Rat saying something by tipping his hat?
Page 1	What is Rat doing? How can you tell? What in the picture makes you think that?
Page 2	What is Cat doing? How can you tell? Is it dangerous for Rat to be near Cat? What might happen?
Page 3	What is happening here?
Page 4	What did Rat do? Why did Rat take the hat? (In a previous book, Rat, SET 1.1, Cat took the hat from Rat)
Page 5	What is Cat thinking? How is Cat feeling? What happened?
Page 6	Where is Rat going? Why is he going there?
Page 7	What is Cat doing? Where did Rat go?
Page 8	What is Cat looking at? What is Cat thinking?
Page 9	What is Rat doing? How does Rat feel?
Page 10	How does Cat feel? How does Rat feel?

AFTER READING

What does this story make you think about?

Is it safe for Rat to live where he lives? Do cats like rats?

Do you like Rat? Why? Why not?

Do you like Cat? Why? Why not?

Did Rat do the right thing by taking the hat from Cat?

Comprehension Questions

Provided here are a variety of questions to ask your students BEFORE, DURING, and AFTER they read. Some teachers may ask many or all of the questions, some teachers only a few. Often one question alone will yeild a rich and lengthy discussion. Many of these questions can be used as writing prompts as well. Of course, a teacher may decide to ask no comprehension questions at all, making their lesson a strictly phonics one.

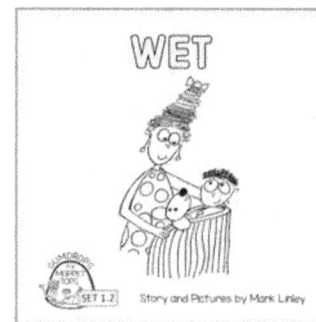

WET

BEFORE READING

Have you ever played with a dog? What did you do?

What do you have to do to take care of a dog?

Have you ever taken a dog out on a walk? What happened?

Why is it important for dog owners to take their dogs out for a walks?

DURING READING

Title Page	What do you think this story is about? What does the front cover make you think about?
Page 1	Why do people like to pet dogs? Why do dogs like to be pet? Have you ever pet a dog?
Page 2	How does the dog feel when the boy takes out the leash? What is the dog thinking?
Page 3	What do dogs do when they go out for a walk?
Page 4	What is happening in this picture?
Page 5	If you meet a dog that you do not know and you want to pet the dog, what should you do first? (Ask the owner if you can pet the dog, ask if it is a friendly dog, a dog that won't bite) Have you or someone you know ever been bitten by a dog? What happened?
Page 6	What is happening here?
Page 7	Why does the boy turn around? How does the boy feel? How does the dog feel? How do you know? Why do they feel this way? If you got caught in the rain would you turn around?
Page 8	Now how does the boy feel? Why? What is the boy thinking?
Page 9	What does the mom think about her son being soaked with rain?
Page 10	How does the boy, his mom, and the dog feel now? Why?

AFTER READING

How did the boy's feelings change in this book?

Do your parents (or grandparents or other family members) worry about you?

Would your mom or dad be worried about you if you were caught out in the rain?

Do you like to take walks in the rain?

What did you think about as you read this book?

Comprehension Questions

Provided here are a variety of questions to ask your students BEFORE, DURING, and AFTER they read. Some teachers may ask many or all of the questions, some teachers only a few. Often one question alone will yeild a rich and lengthy discussion. Many of these questions can be used as writing prompts as well. Of course, a teacher may decide to ask no comprehension questions at all, making their lesson a strictly phonics one.

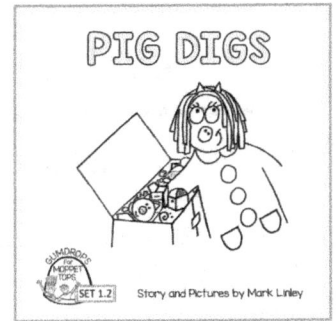

PIG DIGS

BEFORE READING

Do you have a toy box?

Where do you keep your toys?

Do you keep your toys neat and organized and in place or do you keep them in a big jumble?

Can you find your toys when you want to play with them?

Do you sometimes lose your toys?

DURING READING

Title Page	What is the title of this book? What does this title mean? What is Pig doing? What is in this box?
Page 1	How does Pig feel? How can you tell?
Page 2	What do you think Pig is looking for?
Page 3	Do you like to wear wigs? Do you like to play dress up?
Page 4	Now what do you think Pig is looking for?
Page 5	What did Pig find? Do you like to play with dolls or action figures? Do you play with figurines, stuffed animals, or puppets? Do you have a favorite that you like to play with?
Page 6	Now what do you think Pig is looking for?
Page 7	Why does Pig put the same wig on her doll as she wears herself? Do you like to dress up dolls, action figures, or stuffed animals as you dress yourself? Do you know anyone who likes to do so?
Page 8	Now what is Pig doing?
Page 9	What does Pig have now? Do you like music? Do you like to sing?
Page 10	What is Pig doing? Do you like to dance? Do you like music? Would you like to be friends with Pig? Why? Why not?

AFTER READING

What is your most prized possession?

When you play with toy figures (dolls, action figures, figurines, stuffed animals, puppets) what do you pretend?

What do you imagine your dolls, action figures, or stuffed animals can do? What do you say to them? What do they say to you?

Do you play with your toy figures alone? Do you play with them with friends or family?

Comprehension Questions

Provided here are a variety of questions to ask your students BEFORE, DURING, and AFTER they read. Some teachers may ask many or all of the questions, some teachers only a few. Often one question alone will yeild a rich and lengthy discussion. Many of these questions can be used as writing prompts as well. Of course, a teacher may decide to ask no comprehension questions at all, making their lesson a strictly phonics one.

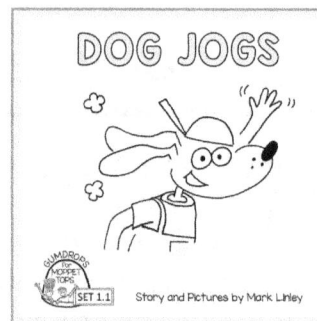

DOG JOGS

BEFORE READING

Do you like to run?

Do you like to skip? hop? jump? gallop? jog? Can you march? slide? creep? stomp? tip-toe? run?

Do you like to race?

Have you ever hurt yourself while running? What happened?

DURING READING

Title Page	What is the title of this book? What is jogging? What good does exercise do for you?
Page 1	What is happening here?
Page 2	Which is faster, running or jogging?
Page 3	What is happening here? Why do Dog's eyes look this way?
Page 4	What is fog? Is Dog in some kind of trouble? What is the problem?
Page 5	Where is Dog?
Page 6	What happened to Dog? Have you ever tripped while running? Why did you trip?
Page 7	What is Dog doing? What is he saying? How does Dog feel?
Page 8	Why did Dog throw the log? How does he feel now? Have his feelings changed? Is the log to blame?
Page 9	How does Dog feel now? What is he thinking?
Page 10	Do you like this ending? Why? Why not? Is there a lesson or moral to be learned from this story?

AFTER READING

What does this story make you think about?

How did Dog's feelings change in this book? Why did they change? Why did Dog get angry?

What other emotions did Dog feel in this book?

Do you get angry sometimes? Why do you get angry?

Does Dog give up? If you try to do something and you don't get it right, what do you do next?

Comprehension Questions

Provided here are a variety of questions to ask your students BEFORE, DURING, and AFTER they read. Some teachers may ask many or all of the questions, some teachers only a few. Often one question alone will yeild a rich and lengthy discussion. Many of these questions can be used as writing prompts as well. Of course, a teacher may decide to ask no comprehension questions at all, making their lesson a strictly phonics one.

SET 1.2 - Book 5

HUG

BEFORE READING

Are there any young children in your family?
When a young child really wants something, what might he or she do to get it?
When you really want something, what do you do to get it?

DURING READING

Title Page	What does the front cover of this book make you think about?
Page 1	How does the girl feel? How does the mom feel? Why do they feel this way?
Page 2	How does the girl feel now? How does the dad feel? Why do they feel this way?
Page 3	What do you think the parents are drinking? What is in the picture that makes you think that?
Page 4	What are the girl's parents doing? What might they be saying to each other?
Page 5	Why is the girl tugging on her parents' pants? What does the girl want?
Page 6	Why are her parents ignoring her? Do you think the girl is rude to be interrupting her parents' conversation? Do you think she has a right to interrupt? In your family are you allowed to interrupt conversations that your parents are having? Are there times when you know that you should not interrupt? When?
Page 7	What do you think is in the jug? What would you like to drink if you were the girl? What is your favorite drink? Is there a drink that you do not like?
Page 8	What is the mom doing? What is she going to do next?
Page 9	Is this what you thought would happen?
Page 10	How do you feel about giving and getting hugs?

AFTER READING

What does this story make you think about?
What was the problem in this story? Was this a big problem or a small problem?
In the end, the girl's parents listened to her. Do your parents listen to you? Do you sometimes feel that your parents don't listen to you? Do they ignore you? If they do, why do they?
If you speak to someone and he or she is ignoring you, how does that feel?
When is it most important to give someone a hug?

Comprehension Questions

Provided here are a variety of questions to ask your students BEFORE, DURING, and AFTER they read. Some teachers may ask many or all of the questions, some teachers only a few. Often one question alone will yeild a rich and lengthy discussion. Many of these questions can be used as writing prompts as well. Of course, a teacher may decide to ask no comprehension questions at all, making their lesson a strictly phonics one.

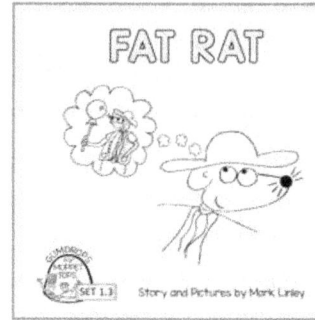

FAT RAT

BEFORE READING

Where do you get your food from? Who makes it?

What are some different places where you can get your food?

Do you like to eat candy or dessert?

Which candy or dessert is your favorite? Is there any candy or dessert that you do not like?

How much sugary food should you eat in a day? in a week?

What is a healthy amount to eat?

DURING READING

Title Page	What is Rat thinking about? If you wanted to eat a lollipop, how would you get one?
Page 1	Do you understand this picture? What is Rat doing?
Page 2	What do you think Rat is going to do?
Page 3	What is Rat carrying? Why is Rat sneaking?
Page 4	What is Cat doing? Why does Rat choose to go out while Cat is asleep?
Page 5	Why must Rat sneak past the cat? What is Rat carrying?
Page 6	What is Rat doing?
Page 7	Do you like lollipops? What is Rat thinking?
Page 8	What is happening here? Is Rat afraid of Cat? Why would he be? Why do you think Cat has a picture of a fish on her wall?
Page 9	What is happening here?
Page 10	What happened? What might happen next?

AFTER READING

How did this story begin? What happened next? Then what happened? How did the story end?

Was the Rat right to take the lollipop?

Do you like lollipops?

What kinds of sweets do you like to eat?

Do you know anyone who does not eat sugar?

What is good about eating sweets? What is bad about it?

Comprehension Questions

Provided here are a variety of questions to ask your students BEFORE, DURING, and AFTER they read. Some teachers may ask many or all of the questions, some teachers only a few. Often one question alone will yeild a rich and lengthy discussion. Many of these questions can be used as writing prompts as well. Of course, a teacher may decide to ask no comprehension questions at all, making their lesson a strictly phonics one.

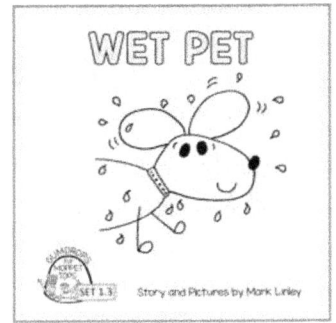

WET PET

BEFORE READING

Do you have a pet? Do you know someone who has a pet?
What do you have to do to take care of pets?
Do different pets have different needs?
If a dog were your pet, what would you have to do to take care of him or her?
What if a cat were your pet? Or a fish?

DURING READING

Title Page	What is the title of this book? What do you think this story will be about?
Page 1	What does this picture make you think about?
Page 2	What is happening here? What is the boy thinking? How does the dog feel?
Page 3	How does the dog feel when the boy lets him off the leash? Why? What is the dog thinking? What will the dog do?
Page 4	Do you think the dog ran through the water on purpose? Why would he do that?
Page 5	How does the lady feel about the dog shaking water on her? What should the mom and the boy say to the lady?
Page 6	What is happening here?
Page 7	How is the dog feeling?
Page 8	What is happening here? What is the boy thinking? How is he feeling?
Page 9	What happened?
Page 10	How does the boy feel now? Do you think this fountain was dangerous for the dog?

AFTER READING

How did this story begin? What happened next? Then what happened? How did the story end?
How did the boy's feelings change in this book?
Why is it important for dog owners to take their dogs out?
Why do dog owners keep their dogs on leashes? Why is it important sometimes to let a dog off a leash?
Have you ever been to a dog park?
If you could have a pet, what animal would it be?

Comprehension Questions

Provided here are a variety of questions to ask your students BEFORE, DURING, and AFTER they read. Some teachers may ask many or all of the questions, some teachers only a few. Often one question alone will yeild a rich and lengthy discussion. Many of these questions can be used as writing prompts as well. Of course, a teacher may decide to ask no comprehension questions at all, making their lesson a strictly phonics one.

SET 1.3 - Book 3

BIG DIG

BEFORE READING

Do you like to dig with a shovel?
Have you ever found anything while digging?
When people dig, what do they sometimes find underground?

DURING READING

Title Page	What does this picture make you think about? Why is pig dressed this way? Why do shovellers wear boots?
Page 1	What do you think Pig is planning to do? What makes you think that?
Page 2	What is Pig doing with her wig? Why is she doing this?
Page 3	Do you think it's hard work to dig a hole?
Page 4	What did Pig find? How did this bone get underground?
Page 5	Now what is Pig doing?
Page 6	What did Pig find? Is this a very deep hole? How do you know? What kind of animal could such a big bone come from?
Page 7	How is Pig feeling?
Page 8	What did Pig find? How does she feel? Why does she feel this way?
Page 9	What is this? What did Pig do? How did the dinosaur skeleton get there? How is Pig feeling now?
Page 10	What do you think of this ending? Why did pig put a wig on the dinosaur skeleton? Would a real dinosaur archeologist put a wig on her discovery? Do you like this ending? Is it silly? Funny? What does this ending say about Pig?

AFTER READING

What does this story make you think about?
What will Pig do next with the skeleton? What would you do with it?
Do you like Pig? Would you like to be Pig's friend? What adventures would you like to go on with Pig?
If you could go on any adventure, what would it be? What discoveries would you like to make?
What adventures have you already had? What discoveries have you made?

Comprehension Questions

Provided here are a variety of questions to ask your students BEFORE, DURING, and AFTER they read. Some teachers may ask many or all of the questions, some teachers only a few. Often one question alone will yeild a rich and lengthy discussion. Many of these questions can be used as writing prompts as well. Of course, a teacher may decide to ask no comprehension questions at all, making their lesson a strictly phonics one.

HOP

SET 1.3 - Book 4

HOP

BEFORE READING

Do you remember when you were two or three years old?

Do your parents (or other family members) tell you stories about yourself when you were younger than you are now? What are those stories?

Do your parents tell you stories about themselves when they were very young? What stories?

DURING READING?

Title Page	Are there any young children in your family? Do they like to jump and hop around? Do you like to jump and hop around?
Page 1	What is happening here?
Page 2	Where are the Dad and his daughter going? How can you tell? Is there a clue in the picture? Do you like to go food shopping?
Page 3	What is the girl doing?
Page 4	What does the girl want? Does your mom or dad let you buy whatever you want?
Page 5	What is the girl doing? What does she have in her hand? How did she get her drink?
Page 6	Who is this? What is her job? What is the girl's father thinking?
Page 7	What do you think of this girl? Do you know any young children? How are they similar to this girl? How are they different? Do their parents let them run around in stores? Do you run around in stores?
Page 8	What is happening here?
Page 9	Why did the can spray out and spill?
Page 10	How does the girl feel? How does her dad feel? What is the girl thinking? What is the dad thinking? Who is the guy with the mop? If you were the girl, what would you do next? If you were the father, what we would you say to your daughter?

AFTER READING

What does this story make you think about?

How did the girl's thoughts and emotions change in this story? How did the father's thoughts and emotions change?

Have you ever spilled anything at a store or at a place that was not your home? At a friends house? At a restaurant? What happened?

If your could talk to this girl, what would you say to her? What would you say to her father?

How could this story have turned out differently?

Comprehension Questions

Provided here are a variety of questions to ask your students BEFORE, DURING, and AFTER they read. Some teachers may ask many or all of the questions, some teachers only a few. Often one question alone will yeild a rich and lengthy discussion. Many of these questions can be used as writing prompts as well. Of course, a teacher may decide to ask no comprehension questions at all, making their lesson a strictly phonics one.

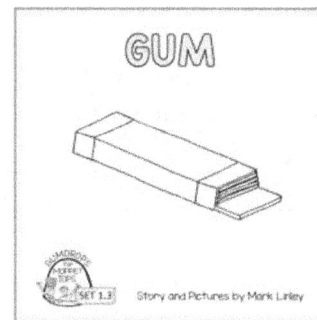

GUM

BEFORE READING

What sweets do you like to eat?

What sweets do your friends and family like to eat?

Do you know anyone who does not like sweets?

Are sweets healthy, or not?

How much sugary food is a fair amount for a kid to eat in a single day? In a week?

DURING READING

Title Page	What is this? Do you chew gum? What flavors do you like?
Page 1	What is the girl doing? What is she saying?
Page 2	Do you share snacks with other people? Do other people share snacks with you? Are there times when it is not a good idea to share food?
Page 3	What might the girls be thinking?
Page 4	Can you hum? Why do people hum?
Page 5	Can you blow a bubble?
Page 6	Is it polite to make chewing noises while you are chewing gum? Is it polite to chew with your mouth open? What are the girls doing? What are they feeling?
Page 7	What is happening here?
Page 8	If you could talk to these girls, what would you say?
Page 9	What are the girls doing? Do they look happy? Why are they happy?
Page 10	Would you take the gum? If you did not like gum, would you still take it? Why then would you take it? If you did not take the gum, what do you think these girls would say to you?

AFTER READING

What does this story make you think about?

Are you allowed to chew gum at home? Are you allowed at school?

Tell us about something nice that you have done for someone else.

Why is it important to be kind to other people?

What makes a good friend?

Is there a lesson to be learned from this book?

INDEPENDENT PRACTICE WORKSHEETS

NAME

_____

- -

_____

DIRECTIONS: Retell the story, trace and write the words.

TRACE   WRITE

1.

2.

3.
 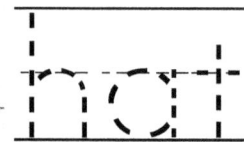

4.
 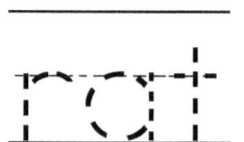

5.
 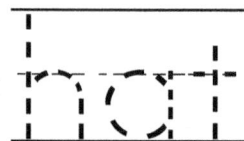

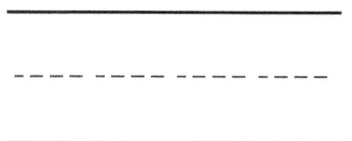
bartlebysbox.com

RAT

NAME _____

DIRECTIONS: Retell the story, trace and write the words.

TRACE   WRITE

6.

   sat

7

   hat

8.

   hat

9.

cat

10.

   hat

bartlebysbox.com

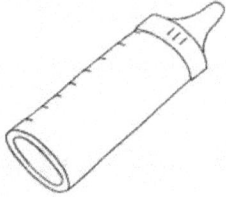
FED

NAME

DIRECTIONS: Retell the story, trace and write the words.

TRACE   WRITE

1.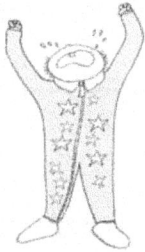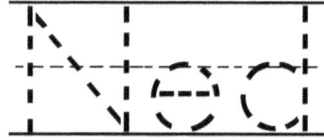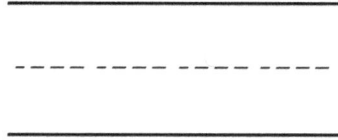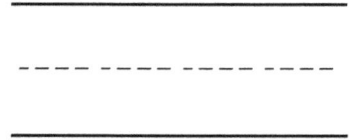

2.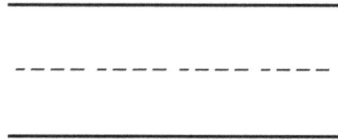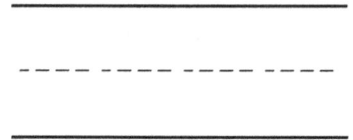

3.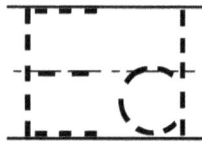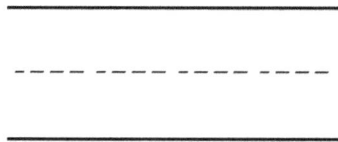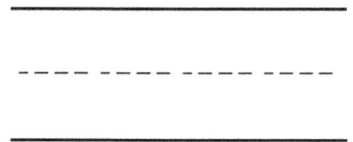

4.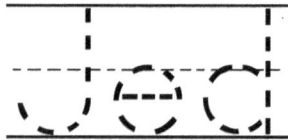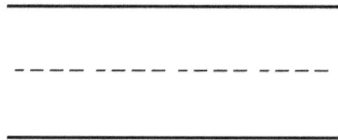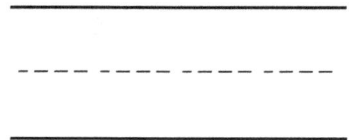

5.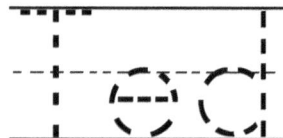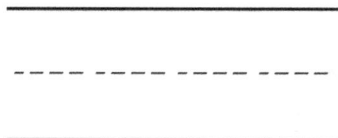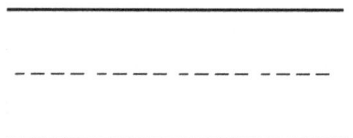

bartlebysbox.com

FED

NAME

DIRECTIONS: Retell the story, trace and write the words.

TRACE	WRITE

6.    Ned

7.    Ed

8.   Jed

9.    fed

10.    bed

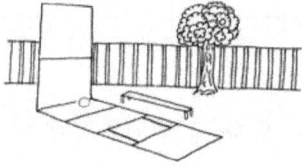

HIT IT

NAME

DIRECTIONS: Retell the story, trace and write the words.

TRACE   WRITE

1.

sit

2.

sit

3.

sit

4.

sit

5.

hit

SET 1.1 - Book 3
GUMDROPS FOR MOPPET TOPS
Copyright © 2017 by Mark Linley. All Rights Reserved. MADE IN THE USA
115

bartlebysbox.com

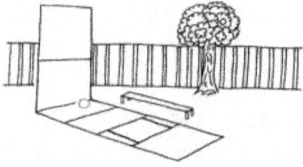

NAME _____

_____

DIRECTIONS: Retell the story, trace and write the words.

TRACE	WRITE

6.

 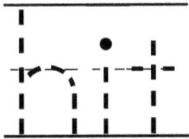 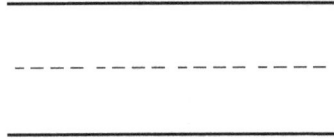 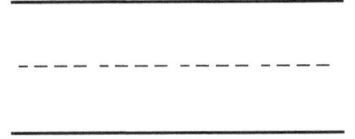

7.

 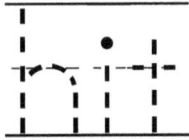 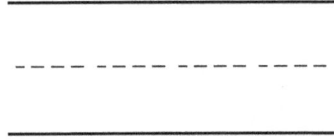 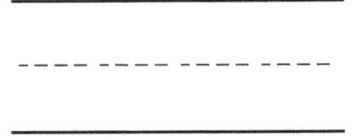

8.

 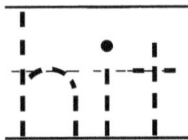 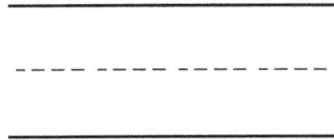 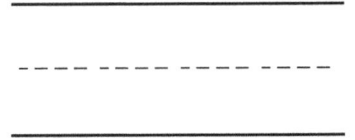

9.

 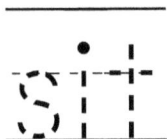 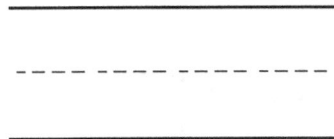 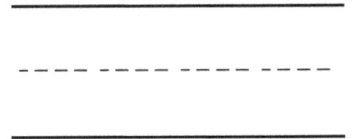

10.

 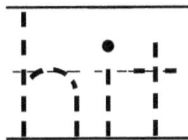 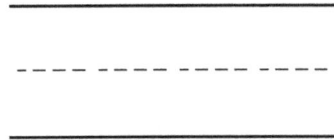 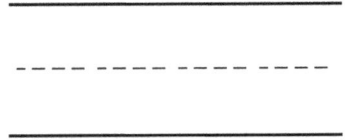

SET 1.1 - Book 3
GUMDROPS FOR MOPPET TOPS
Copyright © 2017 by Mark Linley. All Rights Reserved. MADE IN THE USA

bartlebysbox.com

MOM

NAME

DIRECTIONS: Retell the story, trace and write the words.

TRACE   WRITE

1.

Mom

2.

Tom

3.

Mom

4.

Mom

5.

Tom

SET 1.1- Book 4
GUMDROPS FOR MOPPET TOPS
Copyright © 2017 by Mark Linley. All Rights Reserved. MADE IN THE USA

bartlebysbox.com

MOM

NAME

DIRECTIONS: Retell the story, trace and write the words.

TRACE   WRITE

6.

Tom

7.

Mom

8.

Mom

9.

Tom

10.

mmm

bartlebysbox.com

SUN

NAME

DIRECTIONS: Retell the story, trace and write the words.

TRACE		WRITE

1.

fun

2.

sun

3.

sun

4.

fun

5.

run

SET 1.1 - Book 5
GUMDROPS FOR MOPPET TOPS
Copyright © 2017 by Mark Linley. All Rights Reserved. MADE IN THE USA

bartlebysbox.com

SUN

NAME

DIRECTIONS: Retell the story, trace and write the words.

TRACE   WRITE

6.

run

7.

fun

8.

fun

9.

sun

10.

fun

HAT

NAME

DIRECTIONS: Retell the story, trace and write the words.

TRACE   WRITE

1.

rat

2.
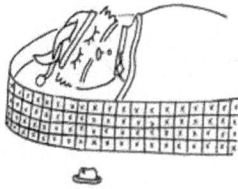

cat

3.

hat

4.

hat

5.

cat

bartlebysbox.com

HAT

NAME

DIRECTIONS: Retell the story, trace and write the words.

TRACE   WRITE

6.

hat

7.

cat

8.

mat

9.

hat

10.

rat

bartlebysbox.com

WET

NAME

DIRECTIONS: Retell the story, trace and write the words.

TRACE   WRITE

1.

 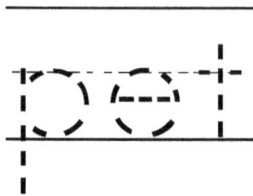

2.

 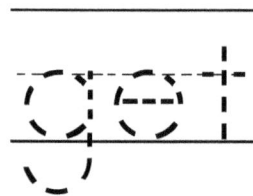

3.

 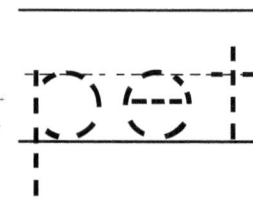

4.

 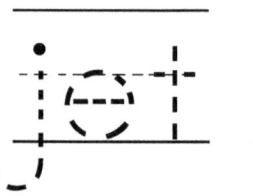

5.

 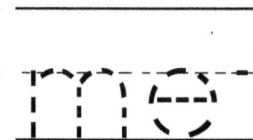

SET 1.2 - Book 2
GUMDROPS FOR MOPPET TOPS
Copyright © 2017 by Mark Linley. All Rights Reserved. MADE IN THE USA
123

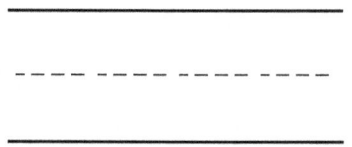
bartlebysbox.com

WET

NAME

DIRECTIONS: Retell the story, trace and write the words.

TRACE   WRITE

6.

wet

7.

wet

8.

let

9.

wet

10.

set

PIG DIGS

NAME _____

DIRECTIONS: Retell the story, trace and write the words.

TRACE   WRITE

1.

pig

2.

dig

3.

wig

4.

dig

5.

pig

SET 1.2 - Book 3
GUMDROPS FOR MOPPET TOPS

bartlebysbox.com

PIG DIGS

NAME

DIRECTIONS: Retell the story, trace and write the words.

TRACE   WRITE

6.

dig

7.

wig

8.

dig

9.

big

10.

jig

SET 1.2 - Book 3
GUMDROPS FOR MOPPET TOPS
Copyright © 2017 by Mark Linley. All Rights Reserved. MADE IN THE USA

bartlebysbox.com

 DOG JOGS

NAME

DIRECTIONS: Retell the story, trace and write the words.

TRACE   WRITE

1.
   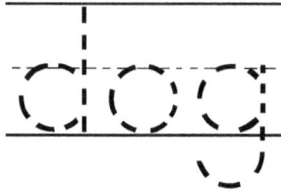 dog

2.
   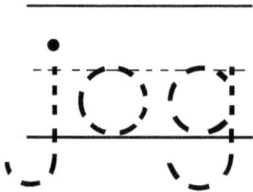 jog

3.
   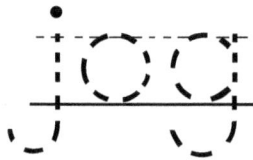 jog

4.
   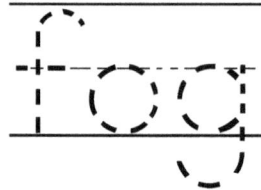 fog

5.
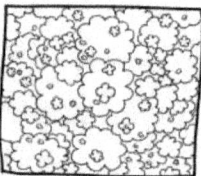   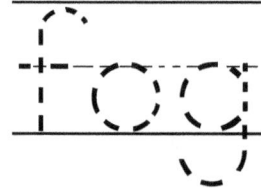 fog

SET 1.2 - Book 4
GUMDROPS FOR MOPPET TOPS

bartlebysbox.com

DOG JOGS

NAME

DIRECTIONS: Retell the story, trace and write the words.

TRACE	WRITE

6.

 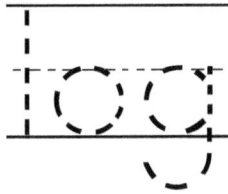 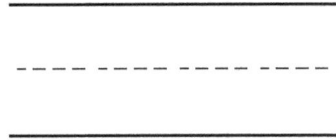 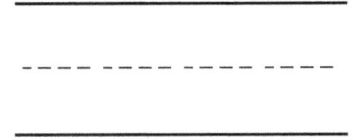

7.

 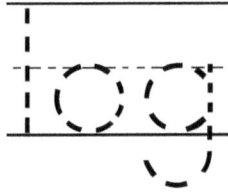 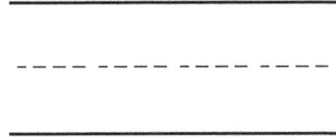 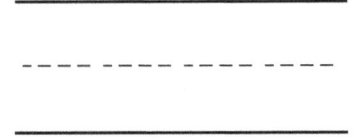

8.

 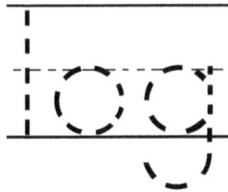 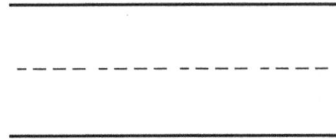 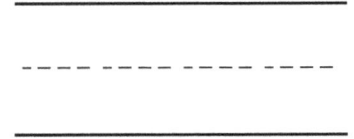

9.

 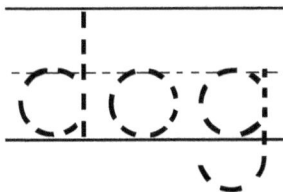 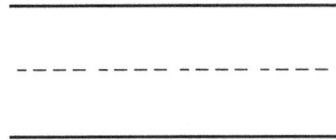 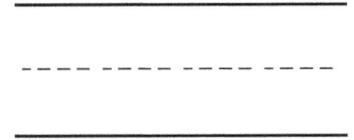

10.

 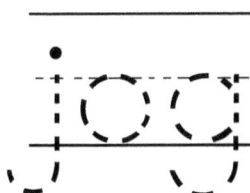 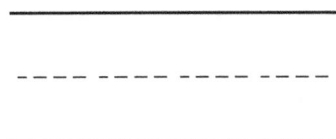 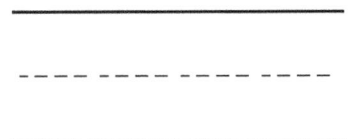

bartlebysbox.com

HUG

NAME

DIRECTIONS: Retell the story, trace and write the words.

TRACE · · · WRITE

1.  hug

2.  hug

3.  mug

4.  mug

5.  tug

SET 1.2 - Book 5
GUMDROPS FOR MOPPET TOPS
Copyright © 2017 by Mark Linley. All Rights Reserved. MADE IN THE USA
129

bartlebysbox.com

HUG

NAME

DIRECTIONS: Retell the story, trace and write the words.

TRACE   WRITE

6.

tug

7.

jug

8.

jug

9.

mug

10.

hug

SET 1.2 - Book 5
GUMDROPS FOR MOPPET TOPS
Copyright © 2017 by Mark Linley. All Rights Reserved. MADE IN THE USA

bartlebysbox.com

130

FAT RAT

NAME

DIRECTIONS: Retell the story, trace and write the words.

TRACE   WRITE

1.
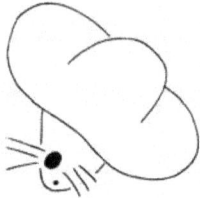
hat

2.

rat

3.

rat

4.
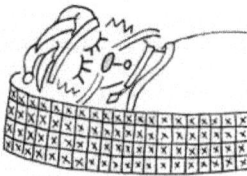
cat

5.

cat

SET 1.3 - Book 1
GUMDROPS FOR MOPPET TOPS
131

bartlebysbox.com

FAT RAT

NAME

DIRECTIONS: Retell the story, trace and write the words.

TRACE   WRITE

6.

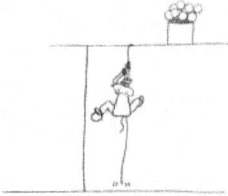

rat

7.

mmm

8.

cat

9.

cat

10.

fat

SET 1.3 - Book 1
GUMDROPS FOR MOPPET TOPS
Copyright © 2017 by Mark Linley. All Rights Reserved. MADE IN THE USA

132

WET PET

NAME

TRACE	WRITE

1.

 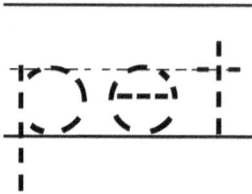

2.

 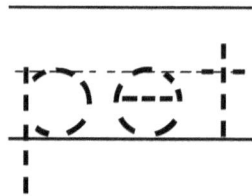

3.

 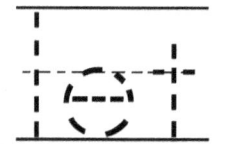

4.

 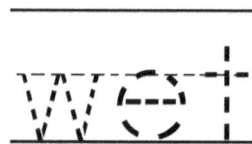

5.

SET 1.3 - Book 2
GUMDROPS FOR MOPPET TOPS
Copyright © 2017 by Mark Linley. All Rights Reserved. MADE IN THE USA

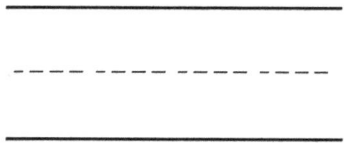
bartlebysbox.com

WET PET

NAME

_____

- - - - - - - - - - - - - - - - - - - -

_____

DIRECTIONS: Retell the story, trace and write the words.

TRACE   WRITE

6.

wet

7.

wet

8.

net

9.

get

10.

pet

SET 1.3 - Book 2
GUMDROPS FOR MOPPET TOPS
Copyright © 2017 by Mark Linley. All Rights Reserved. MADE IN THE USA

bartlebysbox.com

BIG DIG

NAME

_____
- -
_____

DIRECTIONS: Retell the story, trace and write the words.

TRACE   WRITE

1.

pig

2.

wig

3.

dig

4.

big

5.

dig

GUMDROPS FOR MOPPET TOPS

bartlebysbox.com

BIG DIG

NAME

DIRECTIONS: Retell the story, trace and write the words.

TRACE   WRITE

6.

big

7.

dig

8.

big

9.

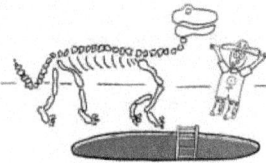

big

10.

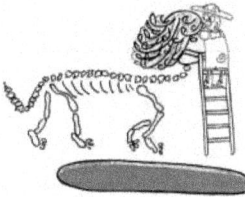

wig

SET 1.3 - Book 3
GUMDROPS FOR MOPPET TOPS
Copyright © 2017 by Mark Linley. All Rights Reserved. MADE IN THE USA

bartlebysbox.com

HOP

NAME

DIRECTIONS: Retell the story, trace and write the words.

TRACE   **WRITE**

1.

   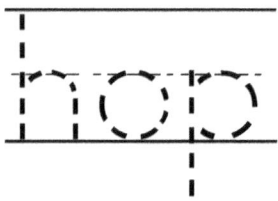

2.

   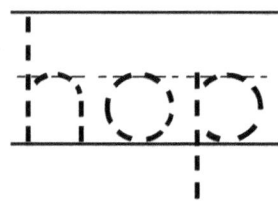

3.

   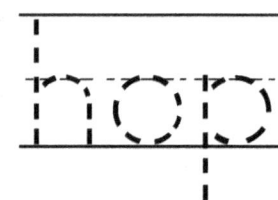

4.

   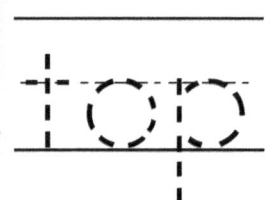

5.

   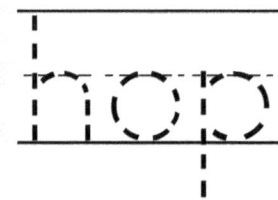

SET 1.3 - Book 4
GUMDROPS FOR MOPPET TOPS

bartlebysbox.com

NAME

DIRECTIONS: Retell the story, trace and write the words.

TRACE   WRITE

6.

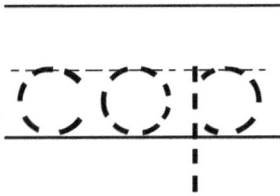

cop

7.

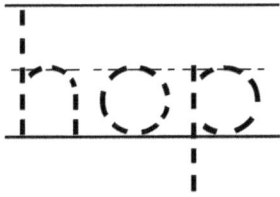

hop

8.

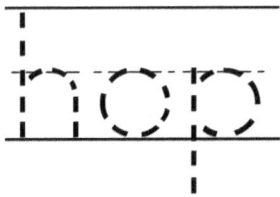

hop

9.

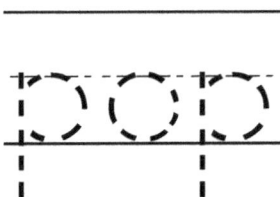

pop

10.

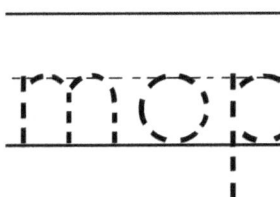

mop

SET 1.3 - Book 4
GUMDROPS FOR MOPPET TOPS

bartlebysbox.com

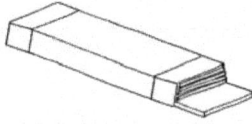
GUM

NAME

DIRECTIONS: Retell the story, trace and write the words.

TRACE WRITE

1.

gum

2.

yum

3.

yum

4.

hum

5.

gum

SET 1.3 - Book 5
GUMDROPS FOR MOPPET TOPS
Copyright © 2017 by Mark Linley. All Rights Reserved. MADE IN THE USA

bartlebysbox.com

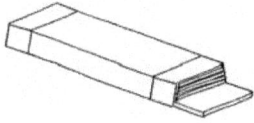

GUM

NAME

DIRECTIONS: Retell the story, trace and write the words.

TRACE   WRITE

6.

yum

7.

gum

8.

yum

9.

hum

10.

gum

www.ingramcontent.com/pod-product-compliance
Lightning Source LLC
LaVergne TN
LVHW061300060426
835509LV00016B/1658